GEORGE WASHINGTON
AND THE AMERICAN MILITARY TRADITION

George Washington in the Uniform of a Colonel in the Virginia Militia
BY CHARLES WILLSON PEALE (1772)
WASHINGTON/CUSTIS/LEE COLLECTION
WASHINGTON AND LEE UNIVERSITY, VIRGINIA, USA

GEORGE WASHINGTON

AND THE

AMERICAN MILITARY

TRADITION

DON HIGGINBOTHAM

MERCER UNIVERSITY
LAMAR MEMORIAL LECTURES
No. 27

THE UNIVERSITY OF GEORGIA PRESS
ATHENS AND LONDON

© 1985 by the University of Georgia Press
Athens, Georgia 30602

All rights reserved

Set in 11 on 13 pt. Linotron 202 Baskerville

The paper in this book meets the guidelines for
permanence and durability of the Committee on
Production Guidelines for Book Longevity of the
Council on Library Resources.

Printed in the United States of America

89 88 87   5 4 3 2

Library of Congress Cataloging in Publication Data

Higginbotham, Don.
George Washington and the American military tradition.

(Lamar memorial lectures ; no. 27)
Bibliography: p.
Includes index.
1. Washington, George, 1732–1799—Influence.
2. Washington, George, 1732–1799—Military leadership.
3. Military art and science—United States—History.
I. Title. II. Series.
E332.17.H63 1985   973.4'1'0924   85-997
ISBN 0-8203-0786-6 (alk. paper)
ISBN 0-8203-0939-7 (pbk. : alk. paper)

For Kathy

Contents

Foreword

WHEN THE NATION LAUNCHED ITS BICENTENNIAL CELEBRA-
tion in the 1970s, Mercer University marked that occasion
by devoting a number of its annual Lamar Memorial Lectures to some aspect of Southern colonial and revolutionary
history. To this end the university was fortunate in bringing
to the campus such distinguished scholars as Clarence L.
Ver Steeg, Jack Greene, and Merrill D. Peterson. With the
approach of 1983, when the glowing memories of the 1976
fireworks were fading, the Lamar Committee considered it
equally appropriate to celebrate the two-hundredth anniversary of the end of the Revolution—the longest war this
country has ever fought.

The committee was supremely fortunate in persuading
the noted historian, Don Higginbotham of the University of
North Carolina, to take a final backward look as we began
to move away from the bicentennial and the events that it
celebrated. With his impeccable credentials as a scholar, his
skill as a writer, and his engaging personality, Professor
Higginbotham's visit to the Mercer campus will long be
remembered, and the present volume will stand as enduring evidence of the thoughtful and stimulating lectures that
he gave to his Mercer audiences on October 24–25, 1983, as
the twenty-seventh Lamar Memorial Lecturer.

In his own introduction Higginbotham has indicated
some concern that he may have gone somewhat beyond the
terms of the Lamar trust in writing about George Washington and the "American" military tradition rather than a

"Southern" tradition. He need not have worried. In dealing with Washington the Southerner and his contribution to the larger American experience he has more than fulfilled all expectations. With great care the author guides the reader through three major phases of Washington's military career: the Virginia period, the tentative opening months of his command at the beginning of the Revolution, and the strenuous years as architect and commander of the Continental army in the later and longer phase of the struggle. With great skill and precision Professor Higginbotham illuminates the complexities of the civil-military tensions present in a democratic society and evaluates Washington's remarkable success in molding a military tradition compatible with and acceptable to such a society. A final chapter analyzes and compares the ideas and careers of Washington and General George C. Marshall and judiciously weighs the military legacy left to the American nation by these towering figures.

Eugenia Dorothy Blount Lamar in her will established these lectures to aid in the permanent preservation of the values of Southern life and culture. By placing his "Southerners" in the larger context of American life, Professor Higginbotham rightly reminds us that Mrs. Lamar has made an invaluable contribution not only to Mercer and to the South but to the whole country.

> Henry Y. Warnock
> for the
> Lamar Memorial Lectures Committee

Preface

THE FIRST THREE CHAPTERS THAT FOLLOW ARE AN EXPANDED version of the Lamar Lectures I gave at Mercer University in October of 1983. Chapter 4 was initially presented at the United States Air Force Academy in March of 1984. It has been revised to serve as a concluding chapter for this volume.* My observations on George Washington and the American military tradition proved to be more timely or relevant than I had intended. That, at any rate, was the opinion of a number of people in the audience at Mercer, for during my days on the Macon campus momentous occurrences involving the American military were splashed across our newspapers and television screens. I refer, of course, to the bombing of the Marine compound in Lebanon and the U.S. invasion of Grenada. Both those events raised questions and elicited discussions on the part of students, faculty, and townspeople who attended my lectures and who responded with courtesy and kindness that I shall always remember.

I wish to express my appreciation to Professor Henry Y. Warnock and other members of the Lamar Memorial Lectures Committee for inviting me to appear as the twenty-seventh speaker in this prestigious series. Special thanks go

---

* "George Washington and George Marshall: Some Reflections on the American Military Tradition," Harmon Memorial Lecture, U.S. Air Force Academy, 1984.

to old friends on the Mercer history faculty, Professors Carlos Flick and Wayne Mixon, as well as to Fran Mixon, for making the hospitality of Middle Georgia a reality for me.

I am also indebted to a number of scholars who graciously offered assistance: Douglas E. Leach, T. H. Breen, W. W. Abbot, James W. Titus, Philander D. Chase, Robert K. Wright, Jr., Russell F. Weigley, Richard K. Showman, E. Wayne Carp, Forrest C. Pogue, Larry I. Bland, and Sharon R. Ritenour. Some read one or more chapters, and some have sharpened my insights in yet other ways; all have saved me from errors of commission or omission.

From my own university, I received substantial assistance. Three of my graduate students—Carol Humphrey, Charles Brodine, and Mark Thompson—supplied a generous portion of aid and counsel. Departmental secretaries Linda Stephenson and Christy Spivey mastered the intricacies of word processing in time to prepare my manuscript with their customary good cheer and efficiency. Dean Samuel R. Williamson, Jr. (and now provost) was instrumental in providing a year's leave following my five-year term as chairman of the history department.

I am grateful to Malcolm L. Call and his fine staff at the University of Georgia Press. Nancy Holmes suggested helpful stylistic changes in the final draft, and Ellen Harris expertly guided the book through the rest of the production process.

I thank my wife, Kathy, and my mother, Maude J. Higginbotham, for favors and kindnesses too numerous to mention. But they will understand my meaning.

DON HIGGINBOTHAM

Chapel Hill, North Carolina
March 8, 1985

GEORGE WASHINGTON
AND THE AMERICAN MILITARY TRADITION

Introduction

SINCE 1983 MARKED THE OFFICIAL END OF THE BICENTENNIAL of the American War of Independence, it seemed appropriate to devote my Lamar Lectures to some aspect of our Revolution that has been permanent and enduring and at the same time to be mindful that this distinguished series was established to widen our knowledge of Southern history and culture. Both objectives could be realized in the theme of the 1983 lectures, which I entitled "George Washington and the American Military Tradition."

Initially, one might well ask whether Washington fits into a Southern version of that tradition. It is a question worth addressing, although not at length. Certainly there were Southerners before the Civil War who spoke of possessing a distinctive martial heritage. Daniel Hundley, in his *Social Relations in our Southern States* (1860), boasted that Southern gentlemen were "most enamored" of army life, which explained why "the South has furnished us with all our great generals, from Washington to Scott."[1] Virginia in particular can claim to be the "Mother of Generals," whose warrior sons include Washington, William Henry Harrison, Winfield Scott, Zachary Taylor, Thomas J. Jackson, Joseph E. Johnston, and Robert E. Lee.

Some historians, sympathizing with these views, have advanced arguments that go somewhat as follows: Southerners, with their rural, agrarian, plantation background, were romantic in temperament, fond of dueling, experienced in

Indian warfare, eager for military commissions, and quick to risk warlike measures. One authority has stated that our struggle for independence was concluded in a Southern style since the revolutionaries were "led to victory by a Virginian experienced in the Indian fighting, and it was in Virginia that Cornwallis surrendered." But if there is anything to the proposition that Southerners "started" the War of 1812, the Mexican War, and the Civil War, it can hardly be gainsaid that Lexington and Concord lacked a Southern flavor.[2]

Nor, on reflection, can we fathom anything peculiarly Southern in Washington's own military experience. True enough, as a young man he had thirsted for glory and a British regular commission in the French and Indian War, but so had ambitious New Englanders and New Yorkers. He had gone so far as to exclaim in his first taste of combat in 1754 that there was something charming in the sound of gunfire, words that remind us of New Yorker Alexander Hamilton's bravado at Yorktown. But there is no reason to believe that Washington was eager for bloodletting and personal military fame more than two decades afterward when he accepted command of the Continental forces. To the contrary, he informed Congress of his great distress. According to Benjamin Rush, Washington confided to Patrick Henry that "from the day I enter upon the command of the American armies, I date my fall, and the ruin of my reputation."[3] The mature Washington was utterly unromantic about human violence in any form; here clearly is an instance of how he had changed from the dashing provincial officer who had flooded General Edward Braddock and his other superiors with pleas for military preferment. As general and later as president he consistently adhered to the notion of war as grim, unpleasant business, a phenomenon to be avoided at all cost so long as the nation's vital interests were not sacrificed in doing so.

Since there is no evidence for the presence of a Southern military tradition during the colonial and revolutionary periods so far as Washington is concerned, one might, albeit perversely, endeavor to stand the theory of Southern distinctiveness on its head: Were Yankees actually more militant than Southerners? During the French and Indian War, Washington himself declared that "Virginia is a Country young in War. Untill the breaking out of these Disturbances has Lived in the most profound, and Tranquil Peace; never studying War nor Warfare."[4] Referring to the same contest, the Massachusetts legislature declared that there was greater enthusiasm for the conflict in New England than in the provinces below the Hudson, "the Inhabitants whereof are but little disposed to and less acquainted with affairs of war."[5] A dozen or so years later John Adams repeated what must have been a widely held New England conception. "Military Characters in the Southern Colonies are few," he opined. "They have never known much of War and it is not easy to make a People Warlike who have never been so."[6] The enormous enthusiasm that characterized the American response in 1775—Charles Royster appropriately calls it the "rage militaire"—was centered mainly in the New England provinces.[7] In the course of the war most native-born ranking generals such as Artemas Ward, Philip Schuyler, Benjamin Lincoln, Nathanael Greene, John Sullivan, Benedict Arnold, Henry Knox, and Anthony Wayne were from states north of Maryland, just as it may be pointed out that most of the significant battles were fought on Northern terrain. In retrospect, however, this evidence adds up to nothing substantial, leaving us to conclude that the military configurations flowing from the eighteenth century were more American than either Northern or Southern.

Washington, of course, was a Southerner but did not realize it—not, at any rate, in the sense that men of Calhoun's generation did and not even to the extent that Jefferson did.

Washington, who sometimes referred to his Virginia as a Middle State, was not oblivious to regional differences among his countrymen. He devoted himself unsparingly from 1775 onward to fostering sentiments of unity in the army and Congress and throughout the fledgling republic. He was the foremost American nationalist of his generation.

It is, therefore, Washington's relationship to those shared components of the American military tradition that should be our focus, although we should point out that, besides the question of Southern distinctiveness, there are other problems with the word *tradition* that require attention before we proceed. Some authorities speak of conflicting militia and professional traditions, of a Jeffersonian-Jacksonian tradition as opposed to an Uptonian one. Still other specialists refer to traditions in terms of strategies: of attrition, of partisan war, of annihilation, and of limited war. So far as the study of Washington is concerned, it is most useful to lump the above aspects together into a complex, multifaceted but nonetheless single American military tradition.

We will be wise to eschew defining all aspects of that tradition, for to grapple with something so broad and at times nebulous would get us into the kind of difficulty that beset those who have sought to delineate a Southern military mindset. We would need to reflect upon temperaments, lifestyles, social values, and other matters that could hardly be considered fully within the framework of these chapters, even assuming that we might agree upon the relevance of such factors and their relationship to American concerns with things military.

The literature that attempts to show the place of individual generals in the American military tradition is rather meager and mostly disappointing. Assuredly such is the status of Washington studies. They have been a subject of interest mainly to professional soldiers, whose works have often been marred by special pleading of one kind or another, usually in behalf of an unrealistically large peacetime military establishment.

The following factors, if not more, are important in a study of the American military experience as it relates to Washington: the character of civil-military relations; the peculiar ways Americans have met their manpower needs in peace and war; the struggle to improve standards and bring about a greater degree of specialization in the officer corps. To these factors we should attach another category, one hard to define and overlapping with those already enumerated. It involves, however imprecisely stated, the challenge of leading officers and men into combat with some sensitivity to their own background and values, as well as waging war itself within the framework of the nation's ideals and the broad goals to be derived from war itself. This element may be what Clausewitz had in mind roughly a century and a half ago when he wrote that war in its various manifestations and dimensions is only an extension of politics.

Though Clausewitz himself displayed scant interest in American history, his famous dictum is well illustrated by two examples from Washington's military life. Washington's first rank was that of major, at only age twenty-one. It was an appointment in the Virginia militia that came on the eve of the French and Indian War in 1753. He received it because of political considerations, for he was allied with the higher echelons of the planter squirearchy that dominated public affairs in the Old Dominion. Twenty-two years later he received a more prestigious commission as commander in chief of the Continental army of the United Colonies, soon to be the United States. He was not naïve about his selection, since he informed several Virginians that he owed it to political factors. The Old Dominion, influential and populous, was needed along with her sister Southern colonies to aid New England, whose forces did not relish the prospect of continuing to resist the legions of British General Thomas Gage without the support of the entire continent. If war and politics are closely linked in most nations—uniquely so in some respects in democratic societies (or perhaps we should say *republican* rather than *democratic* because the American revolutionists themselves would have preferred it)—Washington's colonial and revolutionary military careers offer proof of that linkage in our own history.

My first chapter is devoted to what Washington and the American people experienced in the conduct of war, with both local and professional forces, before 1775. In my second and third chapters, I hope to reveal how Washington was influenced by the knowledge of that experience as commander in chief of the Continental army. My objective in the final installment is to examine Washington's lasting influence on the military tradition that emerged from the colonial and revolutionary years, a tradition that has continued in some measure to guide American military attitudes.

ONE

The Colonial Tradition

IN OUR MIND'S EYE, THE PICTURE OF WASHINGTON THE COLO-
nial military figure is that of the militia officer. Washington,
like other Virginians and indeed like colonials elsewhere,
preferred to be addressed by his military title. From his
middle twenties to the time of the Revolution, he was usually referred to as Colonel Washington. When he posed for
Charles Willson Peale's portrait in 1772—his earliest
known countenance on canvas—he elected to do so in his
old uniform, with its blue coat and red facing, evidently the
same uniform that he donned for sessions of the Second
Continental Congress in the spring of 1775. Although it is
not surprising to see that Peale depicted Washington wearing a sword and gorget, the standard accoutrements of an
eighteenth-century officer, the artist's work includes an item
not found in portraits of British officers of the period. There
is a gun over the Virginian's shoulder, which Douglas S.
Freeman, Washington's distinguished multivolume biographer, believes to be a rifle rather than a musket.[1] Why did
Peale add such a weapon? Was it to signify the importance
of firearms in this New World society for all men, both officers and the rank and file? If Freeman is right about its
being a rifle, there is a real frontier flavor to the portrait.
Long rifles (as opposed to shorter central European mod-
els) were confined to the American backcountry. Probably
first crafted in Pennsylvania, they were the invention of colonial gunsmiths who had responded to the need in hunting

and Indian warfare for a weapon superior in range and accuracy to the musket, which was used by professional
armies with their practice of delivering short-distance volley
fire.

Today, perhaps in keeping with Peale's intent, we may be
tempted to see exemplified in that portrait a colonial military tradition distinct from the professional tradition of the
mother country. We may be all the more inclined to do so if
we think of the specific event of the French and Indian War
for which Washington is best remembered: his bravery during the defeat of British General Edward Braddock's army
near the Monongahela River on July 9, 1755, an army
whose objective had been to seize French Fort Duquesne at
the forks of the Ohio, the location of modern Pittsburgh. He
seems to personify the virtues of forest-wise Virginia fighters as compared to British regulars clad in crimson coats
who were trained to wheel, advance, and give battle in long,
exposed lines three rows deep.

To be sure, Washington and the other Virginians fought
heroically in the Battle of the Monongahela. "I luckily
escapd with[ou]t a wound," he assured his mother, "tho' I
had four Bullets through my Coat, and two Horses shot
under me." Braddock's regulars, surprised and confused by
their foes who assailed them from the protection of wooded
areas, were disgraced, many of them fleeing the scene. We
never saw more than "five or six" of the enemy at any one
time, reported one member of the Braddock expedition,
"and they Either on their Bellies or Behind trees or Runing
from one tree to another." Washington subsequently recalled that "before it was *too late*" he had offered unsuccessfully to take charge of the provincials and engage "the
enemy in their own way." As the afternoon wore on, the
army suffered staggering casualties from a blistering cross
fire. When Braddock's forces began their retreat, Washington assisted in loading the mortally wounded general

into a cart. Then Washington, though still quite weak from a recent illness, traveled throughout the night and part of the next morning to reach the rear guard and supply train, with instructions that provisions, medical supplies, and wagons be hastened forward.[2]

Washington was as proud of the Virginians as he was contemptuous of the redcoats. "The Virginians," he exclaimed, "behavd like Men, and died like Soldier's; . . . I believe that out of 3 Companys that were there that Day, scarce 30 [men] were left alive." The regulars, in contrast, "behavd with more cowardice than it is possible to conceive." It was their "dastardly behaviour" that "exposd" the provincial troops, who "were inclined to do their duty to almost certain death . . . they broke and run as Sheep pursued by dogs; and it was impossible to rally them."[3]

Washington and the other surviving Virginians became heroes in the Old Dominion. "Our Brave Blues" they were hailed, since they wore the customary colonial uniform: blue breeches and blue coats with red facings. According to one story that Virginians doubtless relished in telling and retelling, Braddock, as he lay bleeding on the field, "would cry out my dear Blue's . . . give em tother fire." In the final days before he expired from his wounds, the general "could not bare the sight of a red coat." Upon seeing a regular, "he raved imoderately, but when one of the blues [appeared], he said he hop'd to live to reward em."[4]

A romantic rendition of the French and Indian War deeply embedded in our folklore portrays this battle as proving the superiority of American militia over British redcoats and demonstrating the irrelevance of European military theory and practice in the New World. Actually, the Monongahela disaster only confirmed and reinforced variations on these themes already present in provincial culture. Americans had always believed that militia composed of upstanding citizens were more trustworthy than professional soldiers, who were seen as the dregs of society. Militia were also better fighters because they were motivated by a desire to defend their homes and families rather than by a lust for plunder. The roots of this American militia ethos were imported from England at a time when the Stuart monarchy was turning from a centuries-old militia system to professional soldiers as its first line of defense. Certain seventeenth- and eighteenth-century British writers, who kept alive a radical whig tradition in the parent kingdom and whose works were widely disseminated in America, glorified an English militia that had not effectively existed in modern times and exaggerated the benefits of scarcely trained yeomen in arms because of their dislike and fear of salaried, full-time forces.

Colonial literature abounds with militia themes. In Puritan New England, they often found expression in annual artillery sermons. We discover an example of such thought as early as 1710 in the fledgling colony of South Carolina, where a planter boasted: "If regular troops excell in performing the Postures, . . . militia is much superior in making a true shot. . . . A planter who keeps his body fit for service . . . is doubtless a better soldier . . . than a Company of raw fellows raised in England."[5]

Braddock's devastating defeat brought these sentiments into sharper focus and elevated them as never before to a high level of public approval, if numerous pamphlets and newspaper essays on the subject are reliable indicators. Few were as simplistic in explaining the outcome as the contributor who intoned that redcoats "fight for pay" while Americans take arms "to revenge the Blood of their nearest Friends or Relatives, or to redeem them from a Captive State." Another commentator thought the tragedy lay in the decision not to confine "British Veterans" to garrison assignments, which would have allowed the dispatching of an entire army of colonial "Irregulars" to the Ohio. Perhaps no American penman was more savage in his treatment of Braddock himself than Boston's Charles Chauncy, a Congregational minister, who charged that the general "had no Idea of the *manner of fighting* in use here" and that he had with "great contempt" ignored throughout the campaign the advice of his provincial subordinates.[6] The main thrust of colonial arguments, as Douglas E. Leach summarizes them, was that "Americans, through long experience in fighting both the stealthy Indians and the shrewd French in the wilderness, had developed a special expertise that was neither possessed nor appreciated by the regulars, who supposedly were trained only for open European-style warfare. This idea led slowly but inexorably to another—that under certain favorable conditions a small force of well-armed and woods-wise colonists could rout a much larger, more ponderous formation of professional soldiers. It was an intriguing proposition, not easily forgotten."[7]

With varying degrees of emphasis, according to time and place, the notions that American warfare was unique and hardly required formal training would have a tenacious life. We encounter them just before Lexington and Concord as the colonists praised the advantages of their own militias and deplored the evils of standing armies, particularly the British army currently in their midst. Essayists in the American press reminded Parliament and the king's ministers that a war with her colonies would be for Britain a repeat writ large of Braddock's fiasco in the Pennsylvania wilds. One "Ranger," as he styled himself, explained the Braddock formula in this fashion: the king's regulars would be allowed to land and initially advance without opposition, after which "we can *bush fight* them and cut off their officers very easily, and in this way we can subdue them with very little loss."[8]

Either specifically or by implication parts of the militia ethos found expression during the Revolutionary era in the state constitutions, in the writings of the Antifederalists (and sometimes the Federalists as well), and in the second amendment to the federal Constitution, a part of the Bill of Rights, which states that "a well regulated Militia, being necessary to the security of a free State, the right of the people to keep and bear Arms, shall not be infringed." In the minds of some Americans, the militia ethos was almost as viable in the nineteenth century as in the republic's dawning days. When in 1940 Senator Bob Reynolds of North Carolina warned Hitler not to take lightly American boys who grew up with squirrel rifles in their hands, he implicitly gave testimony to an attitude not wholly dead.

Yet Washington, notwithstanding the Peale portrait and the Braddock campaign, does not lend himself to any personification of the American militiaman. We have explained, of course, why the superficial Washington student might think he should. As we will note later, Washington's duties as commander in chief of the Continental army have prompted still other of his admirers to tie him almost exclusively to a professional military tradition. We will endeavor to demonstrate subsequently that he was not an uncritical apologist for either a militia or a professional ethos.

Truth to tell, Washington never held a high opinion of the militia as an institution, nor did he ever think seriously of himself as a militia officer. He knew that in colonial America there was an enormous gap between the theory and the reality of the militia. Militia training had always fluctuated between being haphazard and being nonexistent. As an organization the militia could hardly be highly effective when it included almost all free white adult males and when officers owed their appointments to their political and social standing. For example, in Frederick County, a frontier area and the scene of much of Washington's French and Indian War activity, the county lieutenant was Thomas, Lord Fairfax, Virginia's only resident nobleman, and the colonel of the Frederick regiment was His Lordship's relative, George William Fairfax.

Had Washington wished to be totally candid, he might have acknowledged the dubiousness of receiving his first militia commission as a major and as adjutant of the southern militia district of Virginia, which meant that he had the responsibility of overseeing the militia training in a wide region of the colony, one distant from his own home. Training days in Virginia as elsewhere were usually honored in the breach and were social occasions as much as anything else when they did occur. A generation before Washington's own military baptism, Governor Alexander Spotswood exclaimed that Virginia's militia was "the worst in the King's Dominions."[9]

Sustained crises, especially the eighteenth-century wars with France and Spain, required the recruiting of special forces, either under the direct control of a colony such as Virginia or as part of an intercolonial army operating alone or in conjunction with a British military expedition. Four companies of Virginians, including Washington's half brother Lawrence who afterward became adjutant for the entire colony, had been among the several thousand provincials who participated in the unsuccessful British attack on the Spanish Caribbean fortress of Cartagena in 1741. The Virginians with Braddock, the heroic blues, also were not militia but rather two companies of rangers and one of carpenters, present because of their skills in woodland warfare. Contrary to contemporary myth, Braddock appreciated those skills.[10]

Washington himself during the French and Indian War was always something between a militiaman and a professional soldier—from his viewpoint decidedly more the latter. In 1754, after Governor Robert Dinwiddie sent Major Washington on his now-famous but fruitless journey to order the French out of the Ohio Valley, Dinwiddie estab-

lished what became known as the Virginia Regiment, to be
recruited from able men, and he chose Washington as lieutenant colonel and second-ranking officer. On the death of
his superior, Colonel Joshua Fry, Washington was promoted
to colonel; however, the regiment was disbanded before the
year's end, and he resigned rather than suffer the humilia-
tion of accepting a lesser rank. It was as a volunteer and
special aid to the general that he had fought with Braddock.
Since the general's defeat and the withdrawal of his remaining redcoats to Philadelphia made it clear that Virginia
would have to defend herself, the colony's leaders reconstituted the Virginia Regiment. Washington once again
agreed to serve, accepting a high-sounding commission as
"Colonel of the Virginia Regiment & Commander in Chief
of all Forces now raised & to be raised for the Defence of
this His Majesty's Colony."[11]

During the next three years (1755–1758), charged with
the task of anchoring the colony's frontier defenses, he labored to make his regiment a first-rate military unit. In this
capacity, he proved to be a good soldier for at least two
reasons. First, he relished a military life. "My inclinations
are strongly bent to arms," he asserted on one occasion; and
on another he voiced his ambition of "pushing my Fortune
in the Military way." Second, he had taken his military education seriously, grasping every opportunity to increase his
"knowledge in the Military Art." He obtained that education by the tutorial method, which was also how doctors
and lawyers learned their crafts in the colonial period. This
tutorial method for soldiers meant discussions with battle-
tested veterans, independent reading, observation, and
firsthand practice. Washington had listened to his brother
Lawrence reminisce about the Cartagena campaign of 1741
with their friend and relative by marriage, Colonel William
Fairfax, who himself had once fought in Spain. He had read
Caesar's *Commentaries;* a translated version of *A Panegyrick to*

the Memory of Frederick, Late Duke of Schomberg, an acknowledged master of the art of European warfare (a book he purchased from a cousin at a cost of two shillings sixpence); and Humphrey Bland's *Treatise of Military Discipline,* the so-called Bible of the British army and affectionately known to generations of officers as "Old Humphrey." On a trip to Barbados with Lawrence he made note of the island's defensive capabilities, including the works of Fort James, a "pretty strongly fortified" post. Part of his firsthand practice in the art of war came before his three-year stint as commander on the Virginia frontier. It began in 1754 when, leading a tiny contingent of men, he tasted the joy of victory over Ensign Jumonville at the Battle of the Meadows and soon afterward felt the pain of defeat when he surrendered Fort Necessity to a superior French party in July of that year. Rarely an indecisive military man, not even at age twenty-two, he had given no thought to retreating before a superior foe. Cool in the face of danger, he never lost his nerve, which his subsequent conduct under Braddock illustrates.[12]

Braddock's campaign not only afforded Washington further experience on the battlefield, but it also gave him the opportunity to witness the day-to-day activities of a professional army. That he was a conscientious observer is indicated by his copying in a small notebook the army's daily general orders for his own edification and future study. Interestingly, Washington eschewed the harsh judgments of Braddock's performance that streamed from his contemporaries and confined his negative comments to the behavior of the enlisted men. He felt that the king's officers had showed courage and disregard for their own safety. (Three decades later he said gently of his old commander that he was "brave even to a fault" and in an orthodox campaign would undoubtedly "have done honor to his profession.") He still in 1755 had enormous respect for the British army.

He had thirsted for a royal commission from Braddock. His persistence in that ambition would influence his subsequent actions, large and small—even to the point of mastering the art of fencing, still one of the social graces for an officer but hardly more than that.[13]

Though not yet twenty-four years of age, Washington had considerable experience in arms when he assumed direction of the reconstituted Virginia Regiment, and he strove to impart that knowledge to his unit through his officers. Had he reflected on the matter, he might have stated that a military leader, regardless of rank, should be a teacher, as he himself would again demonstrate on a wider stage in the Revolution. One of the most valuable lessons that a military commander can impart is a sense of fairness to one and all. Washington's first surviving written address to his officers made that point: "you may . . . depend upon having the strictest justice administered to all; . . . I shall make it the most agreeable part of my duty to study merit and reward the brave and deserving. . . . partiality shall never biass my conduct, nor shall prejudice injure any."[14]

Most of Washington's subordinates would have agreed that the colonel was substantially true to his word, which more than anything else explains why he gained their respect. He had it because of his actions, not because he was an officer, nor even because his was a deferential society in which men looked up to their social and economic betters and the term *gentleman* applied to the few rather than the many. Today officers are entitled to respect because they are officers. Even so, there are varying degrees of regard, determined by the manner in which superior officers conduct themselves. In contrast, the view in Washington's America was somewhat the reverse: the man by his character and performance gave dignity to the office; the office was less likely to give luster to the man. This view may have held particularly true in colonial military services, where squabbling and factionalism seemed to run rampant. Washington implicitly acknowledged the conditions for respect when he cautioned his juniors to "remember, that it is the actions, and not the commission, that make the Officer—and that there is more expected from him than the *Title*."[15]

He repeatedly instructed his field officers and company captains to be proper and correct in dealing with their own subordinate officers and men. Enlistees were to be assured that all promises to provide them with pay, provisions, and equipment would be met on schedule as far as possible. He, like perceptive military leaders throughout American history, pointed out that soldiers performed best under officers they knew and respected. Accordingly, he ordered that recruits "be put under the Command of Officers who enlisted them."[16]

Throughout his public life Washington stressed efficient administrative procedures and high ethical standards of behavior, traits which manifested themselves forcefully during his frontier command. Officers were to keep careful records, providing him with periodic reports of numbers present and absent, of monies on hand, and of supplies and equipment available. Both officers and men who deviated from the straight and narrow felt his retribution. Along with desertion, nothing aroused his wrath like abuse of the civilian population, not only for reasons of humanity but also because his forces depended upon the private sector for countless forms of assistance. In a lengthy document entitled "General Instructions to all the Captains of Companies," Washington declared that his officers' foremost objective was to protect and establish cordial relations with the inhabitants. In this one regard he had been openly at odds with Braddock during 1755. To Washington's mind, the general had displayed little tact or patience in dealing with colonials in all walks of life. Moreover, the years after Braddock's defeat brought more serious Anglo-American tensions as Britain hastened thousands of redcoats to North America. Their needs and their close proximity to colonials led to controversies over quartering troops on civilians, confiscating supplies and equipment, and recruiting servants.[17]

As for tactical training, Washington's ideas were not very different from those of British officers who were his contemporaries. Like most provincial officers, he was less than fully aware that some of his British counterparts had considerable familiarity through both military literature and direct European experience with flexible responses, including guerrilla or partisan warfare. (Historical opinion, in fact, now holds that Braddock himself was no theoretical old-school tactician. He had exercised the necessary precautions for moving a European army through a dense wilderness until the very day of his defeat, when in the afternoon before the battle his staff failed to perform alertly after crossing the Monongahela.) Even so, British ranking officers in the colonies such as Henry Bouquet, John Campbell, earl of Loudoun, and John Forbes after 1755 put new emphasis on training their regulars to shoot at targets, advance over rugged terrain, and respond to surprise attacks.[18]

Washington predictably stressed the value of "bush" tactics for the Virginia Regiment. "I expect you will take great pains to make your Soldiers good marks-men, by teaching them to shoot at Targets," he continually reminded his company officers. These admonitions further undermine the fiction that every American owned a gun and knew how to use it. In the aggregate, however, his sermons and exhortations pointed in another direction: toward British army practices. "For this desirable end," he counseled his officers to read extensively in military literature, beginning with Bland's treatise and then other works "which will give us the wished-for information." He specifically ordered instruction in "the New platoon way of Exercising," by which he meant procedures introduced in the king's forces by the duke of Cumberland.[19] Washington must have known that anything associated with "Billy" Cumberland, the captain general of the British army, would receive a positive response. Triumphant over the Pretender at Culloden and a veteran of the War of the Austrian Succession, the duke had persuaded his reluctant father King George II to hurry royal regiments to the defense of Virginia, although the duke could not be balmed for Braddock's rout. Virginians named in honor of Cumberland a fort, a county, a mountain range, a mountain gap, and a river.

Cumberland might be referred to endearingly as Billy by his rank and file, but he hardly advocated running a military organization by democratic methods; nor did Washington, who early in a subsequent war castigated them as New England ways. "Discipline is the soul of an army," he declared, repeating that time-honored maxim. "It makes small numbers formidable; procures success to the weak, and esteem to all." A disciplined army was also a clean, neatly uniformed army, a conviction Washington emphasized in his regimental communications. To insure that specified drill and ceremonial procedures were correctly followed, "even in the most minute punctilio's," Washington ordered every captain of a frontier fort to send a noncommissioned officer and two enlisted men to his headquarters in Winchester to receive exact instruction, which would then be imparted "on their return" to "the rest of your Command." Not if he could help it would his Virginians resemble the British caricature of colonial soldiers, with their unkempt hair, droopy stockings, carelessly slung weapons, and movements out of step and out of line. The Virginians were, in his eyes, neither militia nor even semiprofessionals; they surely were not to be equated with provincials serving in other parts of America. They *were* professionals because arms was "their profession."[20]

Washington was consciously endeavoring to transform

his Virginians into a force that would be more equal to a British army regiment than any ever raised in English America. He told Governor Dinwiddie of doing things "more after the British Manner," "of pay[ing] that Deference to her Judgment & Experience." As his second-in-command Lieutenant Colonel Adam Stephen confided to Washington, "I think the more our Form resembles that of the Regiments on the Establishment The better pretensions we will have to be Established." The colonel, who had sought from Braddock a royal commission for himself, pressed to have the entire regiment taken into the British army. He could cite a precedent well known to him and other Virginians for such action. His brother Lawrence had received a regular's commission, since the colonial troops recruited for the Cartagena undertaking were royalized and placed under Virginia's Governor William Gooch— "Gooch's American Foot." Washington remembered that, even though the expedition had been a fiasco, Lawrence personally had received most favorable treatment from the governor; Lawrence had been so impressed with the overall commander Admiral Edward Vernon that he had named his Potomac River plantation Mount Vernon.[21]

Long desirous of changing the colors of his coat, Washington had additional reasons for his quest that related to his command of the Virginia Regiment. Twice British captains heading small bodies of men in his operational theater had refused to obey his orders because he held only a Virginia commission. Conflicts over rank and jurisdiction between professional and local forces were not uncommon in the colonial wars, and they would pose recurring problems for American military leaders in future conflicts. Matters came to a head when Captain John Dagworthy, claiming to hold a valid British regular commission and leading Maryland troops at Fort Cumberland on the Maryland side of the Potomac, persisted in thwarting the activities of Washington and his subordinates at a post that was administered jointly by Virginia and Maryland. The Virginians were so sensitive about the issues involved that in 1756 Washington journeyed all the way to Boston to present before General William Shirley the case for placing his regiment on the royal establishment. He carried with him a petition drawn up by his officers, stating that they should not be treated as inferiors to British officers of lower or similar rank, particularly since the Virginians shared equally with regulars the duties and dangers of wartime assignments.

Whatever precedents might be drawn from previous imperial struggles, Shirley felt he lacked the authority to grant Washington's request, though he managed to iron out the dispute at Fort Cumberland in Washington's favor. Washington transparently impressed Shirley, who remarked in a different context to Governor Horatio Sharpe of Maryland that "I know no Provincial officer upon this Continent" so deserving of a high position if an intercolonial force were dispatched against Fort Duquesne.[22] That was, however, small consolation to Washington, who undertook several such efforts on behalf of his officers and himself. The last one in 1757 was directed to Lord Loudoun, Shirley's successor as British commander in chief in America. Washington once again made a lengthy trip, this time to Philadelphia, to see His Lordship. During his interview, Washington presented a brief memorial from his officers, based on a thicker document originally designed to enlist the support of Governor Dinwiddie. This parchment is worthy of attention because it spells out so clearly the officers' perceptions of themselves and of their accomplishments. Some had served since the formation of the original Virginia Regiment in 1754.

They accurately claimed "that the Virginia Regiment was the first in arms of any Troops" in America during the French and Indian War, having completed "three years hard & bloody Serivce." Unlike other troops (in what was obviously a slap at the remnant of Braddock's regular regiments and at British forces in general), they had had no "agreeable recess in Winter Quarters" since "the Nature of the Service in which we are engagd, and the smallness of our Numbers . . . keep us constantly in Motion." But what if it should be said that "the Troops of Virginia are Irregulars, and cannot expect more notice than other Provincials"? At pains to explain that they were not militia, should any confusion exist on that score, militia being part-time or seasonal soldiers, the Virginians could legitimately state that they needed "nothing but Commissions from His Majesty to make us as regular a Corps as any upon the Continent. . . . We have been regularly Regimented and trained; and have done as regular Duty for upwards of 3 Years as any regiment in His Majesty's Service."[23]

When Loudoun rejected the appeal of Washington and his subordinates, we can only imagine their disappointment and frustration. His Lordship did not give a high priority to the Southern frontier and the capture of Fort Duquesne but rather stressed the immediacy of launching an offensive toward the Great Lakes. It must have seemed to Loudoun, who had only recently set foot in America, that he was bombarded by the colonists with an unending stream of requests. For example, approximately one hundred provincials descended on his headquarters and offered to serve as gentlemen volunteers—as Washington had done to Braddock—in order eventually to obtain a king's rank. These provincials included such prominent Virginians as young William Henry Fairfax and William Byrd III.[24]

Yet for Washington, Loudoun's rejection of his appeal was only one of multiple frustrations associated with his frontier command; the others would have been bearable, might even have withered away, had he possessed the authority and resources accompanying a royal commission to back him up. If Washington was a teacher, he was a student as well. Douglas Freeman has written that "recruitment, discipline, and fort building" were, along with British-colonial military controversies, "hard lessons in the school of experience." "I am wandering in a wilderness of difficulties," Washington complained to the House of Burgesses Speaker John Robinson. Responsible for a line of forts stretching over 350 miles, the longest exposed frontier in America, Washington seemed perpetually thin on necessities—first one, then another, and often several at once (clothing, provisions, equipment, arms and ammunition). Reluctant though he was, it became necessary in emergencies to impress from civilians, though as a consequence, "they threaten[ed] . . . 'to blow out my Brains.' "[25]

Most of all, Washington lacked manpower. Although Dinwiddie had boasted to Loudoun that Washington was unsurpassed as a recruiter, the governor had cautioned London officials not to anticipate Virginians' rushing to the colors. The Old Dominion was a colony of freeholders who treasured their independence and resented regimentation. Recruiting lagged so badly that at its low tides the regiment had under four hundred effectives and never reached the fifteen hundred authorized.[26]

Throughout he had to rely on the militia to help occupy distant posts and respond to French and Indian forays. Even at its best, the militia, which Washington always saw as little more than a necessary evil, functioned chiefly as a form of selective service. Men were drafted from their county companies and then were re-formed into new, temporary units while on duty. When they were summoned, Washington always had several concerns: would they be reasonably well armed, would they turn out in adequate strength, and would they remain long enough to be useful? They were invariably minus weapons. One contingent of two hundred Culpeper County men reported with a total of only eighty firelocks.[27] Instead of arriving promptly, militia trickled in, fewer than requested, or ignored the call completely, expressing indifference or fear for their safety. In October 1756, Washington discovered that when one-third of the militia in Augusta County were ordered out, one-thirteenth showed up. At first the militiamen summoned in some emergencies could not be compelled to stay more than thirty days, including the time it took to reach their stations and return home (a process that could absorb half the month). Generally, militia legislation specified that draftees were accountable for longer tours, but the acts of 1756 and 1757 stipulated that they could not be retained beyond December 1 of the year in which they took the field, nor could they be dispatched outside the colony. While numbering twenty-seven thousand men on paper, the colony's militia failed to meet the manpower requirements of the war and were no more effective than efforts "to raize the Dead," according to Washington.[28]

Militia posed other headaches. Often disorderly and insolent, they suffered scant retribution for their ill behavior since they were not subject to the martial law governing the Virginia Regiment. Patterned after the British Mutiny Act, this law passed by the General Assembly authorized the death penalty for desertion, mutiny, and disobedience. After one surprisingly good militia turn-out, a messenger brought a report of the approach of a sizable Indian war party. Before this intelligence proved to be erroneous, several hundred assembled militiamen at Winchester vanished. The express "might as well have ridden down the street shouting that a thousand war-crazed savages were entering the town," wrote Douglas Freeman. "Men . . . pictured themselves as already scalped. . . . they began to pour out of Winchester on the roads to the gaps of the Blue Ridge. With scarcely a pretense of concealment, they deserted en masse."[29]

These irregulars felt, quite correctly, that the uniformed

officers and men of the Virginia Regiment looked down on them. There are habitual tensions when soldiers of dissimilar training and standards are thrown together, as Washington and his Virginians had learned during their prior service with British regulars and as he would be reminded later by friction between Continentals and militia in the Revolution. When a Prince William County militiaman made himself insufferable with his own condescending remarks about "the blues," he was slapped in the guardhouse. His comrades broke in and released him, and then, to show their contempt for superior authority, they "pull'd down the House," said Washington. (It was a typical eighteenth-century gesture of defiance: to take apart piece by piece a structure that symbolized immorality or oppression as the case might be; whorehouses and tax collectors' quarters were ever favorite targets.) The original culprit, feeling his oats after feeling his freedom, now swore that the officers of the Virginia Regiment were a pack of "Scoundrels and that he could drive the whole Corps before him." Washington concluded his account of this episode in tantalizingly brief fashion, although it is obvious that he and his officers looked the other way while an unnamed member of the regiment cured the obstreperous one of his "imprudence."[30]

While most militia did not imitate the violence of the Prince William men, they were scarcely reticent about protecting their interests. Even those that fulfilled their service would rarely stay beyond their calendar date. Nor did they suffer in silence if their basic needs were unmet, if promises could not be kept, if they saw better ways of running an army. "Every *mean* individual has his own crude notion of things, and must undertake to direct," complained Washington. "If his advice is neglected, he thinks himself slighted, abased, and injured; and, to redress his wrongs, will depart for his home."[31]

If these men knew their rights, it was not always because

they were the respectable citizen-militia that inspired idealistic prose in both England and America. Sensitive to con-
stituent pressures, the General Assembly more often than
not restricted drafts to men "not free-holders or house-
keepers qualified to vote at an election of Burgesses." Even
when men of modest or better means were so unlucky as to
have their names pulled from a hat, they were normally per-
mitted to escape service by hiring a substitute or paying a
£10 fee. Consequently, Washington increasingly drew upon
the lowest orders of society, whom he once portrayed as
"loose, Idle Persons that are quite destitute of House and
Home." In time, every form of mankind was recruited,
drafted, or impressed, including elements that mostly fell
outside the militia structure—the "willfully unemployed,"
absconding husbands and fathers, indentured servants, va-
grants, free blacks, and Indians. It was primarily those persons not a part of the organized militia who were con-
scripted into the regiment itself for longer service, but as
always the results for Washington were depressing. One en-
treaty to the Cherokee, for instance, netted seven warriors
and three squaws. This would not be the last American war
in which military commanders would scrape the bottom of
the barrel of human resources.[32]

Why did Virginia's colonial government not act more de-
cisively to win the war on her borderlands? Part of the problem was the frontier nature of the war itself. Most Virginians saw themselves as unaffected by the struggle, which
appeared to be far away and seemingly constituted no real
threat to the Old Dominion. Indeed, as Washington himself
admitted to Lord Loudoun, some felt the conflict had been
unnecessary, precipitated by the expansionist lustings of
Governor Dinwiddie and the Ohio Land Company. Consequently, unwilling to make a less-than-popular war downright divisive, the colony left its productive citizens—the
freeholders—largely alone, except for short-term militia

service, which could usually be avoided. Instead, it con-
scripted men for the Virginia Regiment who had no voice in
political life, or it turned to recruiting soldiers from outside
the Old Dominion, a high percentage of the latter being
foreign-born. Since the flotsam and jetsam of that era had
so little stake in the outcome, and since their pay and treatment under the military code made them literally second-
class citizens in comparison to the militia, it is understandable that enlistments lagged and that desertion rates were
high in the Virginia Regiment. The Reverend James Maury
reported in June 1756 that "no person of any property, family, or worth" had enlisted in the Virginia Regiment.[33]

Small wonder that Washington was not an eternal op-
timist, that his idealism about mankind was more tempered
than that of many American revolutionists. He was ever
mindful of the self-interested dimension in people, which
must have owed something to his failure to secure the voluntary enlistment of responsible citizens in defense of their
own soil during the French and Indian War. Washington
might have concluded his first military career a total cynic
except for a dramatic upswing in his fortunes in 1758. The
years 1755–1757 had been dismal not only for Washington's small command but also for British-American fortunes everywhere. The loss of Oswego on Lake Ontario and
Fort William Henry in New York were coupled with Loudoun's failure to take the French fortress of Louisbourg. But
William Pitt, the new head of the London ministry,
breathed fresh life into the creaky war machinery and dug
liberally into the royal treasure chest in order to reverse the
tide. A three-pronged offensive for 1758 targeted Duquesne,
Quebec, and Louisbourg, with Brigadier General John
Forbes to command the army of regulars and provincials
assigned to drive on the forks of the Ohio.

Here was an opportunity for Washington, always an aggressive, offensive-minded officer destined in both his mili-

tary careers to spend the great preponderance of his days on the defensive. While he had closed the door on all hopes of obtaining a king's commission, he thirsted to accompany Forbes, but in a capacity commensurate with his experience and accomplishments. He urged Brigadier General John Stanwix to "mention" him "in favorable terms" to Forbes as a man far above "the *common run* of provincial officers." Similarly, to Colonel Thomas Gage, a fellow Monongahela veteran, he pleaded for a good word because he had been "much longer in the Service than any provincial officer in America."[34]

Both Forbes and Washington held a generally low opinion of provincial troops, though Washington would have claimed otherwise for the officers and some men of his own regiment, which was designated along with other colonial forces to join the second campaign against Fort Duquesne. Forbes, who characterized American officers as a "bad Collection of broken Innkeepers, Horse Jockeys, & Indian traders," considered Washington a notable exception. So did Forbes's colonels. At their request, he diagrammed a suitable line of march for a heavy column of four thousand men—the approximate number Forbes might deploy—penetrating densely forested country, together with a scheme for promptly forming "an Order of Battle in the Woods."[35]

It is quite likely that Forbes adopted a modified form of Washington's plan in mid-November. After months of back-breaking road-building, the general undertook a race with winter and the calendar as well, since most of his provincials were to be mustered out on December 1. Washington had recommended that three divisions proceed ahead of the main body, and now Forbes made such a disposition of his army, with orders for the three divisions to hack out the remaining portion of the trail and lead the advance on the French stronghold. Washington, the only provincial to head a forward division, commanded the Virginia, North Carolina, Maryland, and Delaware units. But there was no ambush to repulse or battle to be won. The outnumbered French, seeing their adversaries had overcome both weather and wilderness, burned their fort and departed shortly before Forbes's scouting parties arrived.

A campaign that ended anticlimactically had nonetheless appreciably deepened Washington's military knowledge. Forbes commanded the largest army in which Washington had served, and his crisply fashioned general orders dealing with quick assemblages, protection of weapons in inclement weather, inspection of equipment, and so on must have been absorbed by the Virginian with all the care he had devoted to Braddock's instructions. A sound and energetic officer, Forbes had made his mark as an administrator, talented in putting an army together and then maintaining it. So far Washington too had been chiefly an administrator, holding together a scattered wilderness command by dint of husbanding his pitifully inadequate resources. Had Washington perceived his future, he would have seen that his disappointments over missing out on formalized engagements had been more than compensated by his lessons in the Forbes school of management techniques. In any event, he had played a part in realizing his most pressing goal as colonel of the Virginia Regiment: the seizure of the forks of the Ohio, from which the French had spewed out hostile tribesmen to ravage the borders of the Old Dominion.

Washington's second goal, gaining crimson regimentals for his Virginians, had met with failure. It was a disappointment doubtless rekindled by the presence, with Forbes's army, of part of the Royal American Regiment. It takes no imagination to speculate that Washington would have loved to command the Royal Americans or, better still, to have seen his Virginia Regiment given the same status. The Royal Americans constituted the only British regiment (officially, the 6oth Foot) composed largely of provincials, although the colonists were frozen out of the officer ranks, a circumstance that must have rankled Washington and his Virginia officers. Even so, Douglas Freeman may not have exaggerated in claiming that the veteran commander of the Royal Americans, Colonel Henry Bouquet, both "by temperament and training . . . probably was second only to Forbes among all the soldiers from whom Washington could learn."[36]

Washington and Bouquet shared one soldierly quality, the ability to engender a strong esprit de corps in their officers. That sense of oneness among the Virginians was owing to a number of things, including Washington's persistent labors to secure them regular status, his eagerness to defend them from critics in Williamsburg, his striving to meet their material needs, and his fair and impartial treatment of them. Although there is considerable evidence of the officers' esteem for him, that esteem was manifested most poignantly at the close of 1758. With Duquesne taken, with a royal commission apparently forever beyond his grasp, with marriage beckoning, and with a seat in the House of Burgesses awaiting him, Washington resigned his commission in the service of Virginia. We find high regard expressed in the "Humble Address" signed by officers of his regiment as Washington took leave of them. "Judge . . . how sensibly we must be Affected with the loss of such an excellent Commander, such a sincere Friend, and so affable a Companion," they wrote. Though obviously aware that his decision was final, they could not help adding that "your Presence only will cause a steady Firmness and Vigor to actuate in every Breast . . . while led on by the Man we know and Love."[37] To our ear, the prose is stilted and effusive, but the substance is worth our reflection. It is high praise in any language, particularly for a twenty-six-year-old provincial officer. No doubt any officer, then or now, would find it intensely rewarding to be so regarded by those he had led in the field.

Captain Robert Stewart, a Scot who had been with Washington throughout the war (including the Braddock campaign when the two colonials had helped the mortally wounded commander from the field), wrote Washington in after years: "I think without vanity we can assert that there never was and very probably never will be such another Provincial Regiment." Stewart was undoubtedly correct. Washington, the teacher, had succeeded in spite of adversity. His young officers—almost wholly innocent of military lore in the beginning, according to Dinwiddie—had gained the esteem of Forbes and Bouquet. His enlisted men also had performed ably. "The General has complimented me publickly on their good behavior," he boasted to Governor Francis Fauquier, Dinwiddie's successor. Forbes's "Highlanders and . . . [the Virginia troops] are become one People, shaking each other by the hand wherever they meet."[38]

In fact, during the Forbes expedition Washington had finally operated with a full regiment. He was able to do so because Virginia, promised subsidies by William Pitt, abandoned conscription, "the cornerstone" of its defensive policy since 1754; instead, it offered liberal bounties for voluntary enlistments in 1758 and thereafter. As the Reverend Samuel Davies approvingly stated in a sermon, Virginians were no longer coerced into taking up arms but could now make their own choice as free men.[39]

Yet it would do an injustice to Washington—and to his soldiers—to deny that his own persuasiveness had bound some of the rank and file to the regiment before enlistments or reenlistments became more financially attractive in 1758. Regardless of their social backgrounds or their perception of Virginia's war aims, some of the men voluntarily stayed with Washington. They persevered in spite of conditions, and in doing so they maintained the integrity of the regiment. If these "blues" were as poor and devoid of property as contemporaries claimed, and if the conflict stemmed from expansionist impulses of a portion of the elite, then Washington could hardly press upon them the notion that theirs was a "glorious cause," as he did quite justifiably in his exhortations to Continental troops in the Revolution. He and the other officers could stress what might be termed a professional ethic, an idea which requires elucidation at this juncture. Such an ethic seems to have been a factor in the steady improvement of the regiment in the year before the Forbes campaign. When two companies were temporarily dispatched to Charleston, South Carolina, in 1757, they found—according to Captain George Mercer—that they were "looked upon in quite another Light by all the [British] Officers than we were by Genl Braddock. . . . we have been told by the Officers that nothing ever gave them such Surprise as our Appearance . . . . , for expecting to see a Parcel of ragged disorderly Fellows headed by Officers of their own Stamp (like the rest of the Provincials they had seen) behold they saw Men properly disposed who made a good & Soldier like Appearance and performed in every Particular as well as could be expected from any Troops." And as for the Virginia officers, their royal counterparts were impressed by their appearance as well as by their leadership, possessing as they did "Sash & Gorget with a gentell Uniform, a Sword properly hung, [and] a Hat cocked." Lieutenant Colonel Adam Stephen was equally proud of the Charleston-based contingent, which he commanded. His comments about their tactical abilities indicate that Washington's training—a combination of European and American methods—had paid off. His troops were as "well disciplin'd" as any regular units in North America. Furthermore, they knew "parade [formations] as well as prussians, and the fighting in a Close Country as well as 'Tartars'."[40]

Stephen might have added that a unit whose performance improves because of its training will in turn bring out the best in its members as individuals, including a sense of pride in being part of a respected fighting force. That, in brief, is a professional ethic. Washington would have concurred had Stephen simultaneously acknowledged that noncommissioned officers also contributed substantially to unit cohesion. There were sergeants who put in years with the regiment and in time became officers themselves. One should eschew easy generalization about military behavior and socio-economic status, an opinion confirmed by a recent study showing that many Massachusetts recruits in the French and Indian War whose names did not turn up in tax and property records nonetheless made good soldiers.[41]

The Virginia Regiment continued to give a good accounting of itself in the years before it was disbanded in 1762. Brigadier General Robert Monckton, heading British forces in the Southern colonies, assured his superior General Jeffery Amherst that the Virginia Regiment performed its "Duty as well as any old Regiment" on the royal establishment. The credit for its "distinguished character," according to Captain Stewart, was owing to Washington's "Military Talents," even though Washington had retired from the profession of arms. The former colonel continued to follow the regiment's campaigning with understandable pride, as his correspondence reveals.[42]

There is irony in the awareness that some Englishmen and Virginians probably considered Washington's retirement no severe loss either to Britain or to America. Since he had demonstrated fine ability under arms, that might seem like an unfair opinion. However, he had evinced scant sympathy or understanding for the problems of his superiors, both civilian and military. Washington was too quick to blame others for obstacles not easily overcome in a backwoods conflict marked by human and material shortages, home-front discord, inadequate governmental machinery, and jurisdictional conflicts between the colonies themselves and between the provincials and the home government.

Washington the soldier became exceedingly political in his behavior. Once close to Governor Dinwiddie, who had boosted his career at every opportunity, Washington was mainly responsible for the chill that enveloped their relationship. When the colonel did not get satisfaction from the governor—when he felt Dinwiddie did not respond properly to his difficulties—he circumvented him by dashing off letters at times critical of the chief executive to leaders of the General Assembly, including Councilor William Fairfax and House Speaker John Robinson, who was also treasurer of the colony.[43]

Up to a point, Washington's epistolary energies might have been defensible, for in reality war-making authority was divided in colonial Virginia, just as it has been in the United States under the federal Constitution. Such divisions have always generated conflicts over control of military matters and the overall governmental war powers. In Virginia and the other colonies, however, the military role of the legislatures grew in an evolutionary manner, the result of protracted and expensive eighteenth-century imperial conflicts. As governors requested swollen sums for militias and semiprofessional forces such as Washington's regiment, American provincial legislatures demanded in return a hand in scrutinizing campaign expenditures and insisted on a voice in still other areas that London officials had considered the preserve of royal executives. In Virginia, these precedents were firmly implanted before the governorship of Dinwiddie, who reluctantly agreed to a joint committee of the Council and the Burgesses overseeing appropriations.[44] Therefore, it was not unreasonable, in the absence of any instructions to the contrary from Dinwiddie, for Washington to keep powerful provincial leaders abreast of military developments and his regiment's requirements.

Doubtless Washington himself realized that the balance of power in Virginia had shifted to the lower house of assembly. Likewise, he must have concluded early in the conflict that his regiment had no political constituency, as did the militia, composed as it was of the electorate. Given those circumstances, he could hardly avoid being a lobbyist for his command along with executing his overwhelming responsibilities in the field.

Furthermore, most of the concerns that Washington penned to Fairfax and Robinson were addressed to Dinwiddie as well. But the colonel was sorely at fault in casting aspersions on the governor's character and ability in communicating to the legislative chieftains. He asserted that Dinwiddie's unresponsiveness was partly personal in nature— that the governor appeared to wish to discredit him. To the speaker he confided on December 19, 1756, "My Orders are dark, doubtful, and uncertain; *to day approved, to-morrow condemned*: Left to act and proceed at hazard: accountable for the consequences; and blamed, without the Benefit of defense!"[45] We can, of course, endeavor to find some extenuating circumstances in this situation. The governor and the colonel were separated in more ways than one: by a thirty-nine-year age difference and by the perspectives of frontier Winchester and tidewater Williamsburg. Still, one must conclude that Washington's behavior was far from admirable.

Equally indefensible were his behind-the-back barbs at both executive and legislative branches. Military men in free and open societies are not infrequently provoked by the slowness and awkwardness of what has become known as the democratic process, even when they acknowledge—in theory, at any rate—their commitment to civil control.

Washington displayed this irritation in what he might have styled a soldier-to-soldier letter to Lord Loudoun in 1757. He complained of the dearth of military know-how on the part of his political masters in Williamsburg, where, he might have added, he was required to journey periodically to explain and justify his accounts and other matters, where too he had been on the receiving end now and then of harsh and probably unfair remarks about his own performance and about the conduct of certain of his officers and men.[46] These "Chimney Corner Politicians," as he labeled them, were cautious to a fault, having given "no regard hitherto . . . to my remonstrances" on various issues. Even in extreme emergencies, the lawmakers had bowed to the people's insistence on putting their personal freedom ahead of the order and regimentation essential to choke off the Franco-Indian peril. Only stern, far-reaching legislation dealing with the military's sometime need to impress goods, quarter troops on civilians, and augment the authority of courts-martial could bring victory. Without such laws, he had reluctantly and as a last recourse taken extralegal measures in the defense of the colony; but the lawmakers, excessively "tenacious of Liberty," were "prone to Censure; [and] condemn all Proceedings that are not strictly Lawful, never considering what Cases may arise to make it necessary and excusable."[47]

Since Loudoun himself had been accused by provincial legislatures of imperious and dictatorial conduct, he likely had some feeling for Washington's view of political bodies. In any event, the colonel found a defender of what might be called his less-than-respectful attitude toward civil control in the person of Richard Bland, a highly regarded veteran legislator and prolific essayist from Prince George County. Bland evidently expressed himself in a now-missing issue of the *Virginia Gazette* in 1756, his remarks prompted by criticisms of Washington appearing previously in that same newspaper. Bland voiced an opinion of civil-military relations that would occasionally surface in the course of American history, though never gaining wide acceptance. In moments of crisis, he warned, "Generals and Commanders of Armies must be left to act as they find it most expedient for their Country's Interest." Whatever the merits of "shake-[ing] off all restraints," as Bland phrased it, the legislature failed to adopt the more aggressive measures that he advocated, with the result that he wrote Washington the following year of his continued displeasure with his fellow burgesses.[48]

Judging from the openness with which Washington's own staff revealed to him their hostility toward their civilian superiors, it seems reasonable to assume that the colonel scarcely discouraged what at a later time would be seen as both potentially dangerous and unethical behavior. "How infatuate are our Assemblies!" exclaimed his secretary John Kirkpatrick, "heedless to the reports of Danger, and indifferent in their measures for the General safety."[49]

Yet Washington also exhibited the ability of cozying up to Virginia politicians at the expense of a British general—in this instance, John Forbes, whom Washington indiscreetly faulted to Dinwiddie's successor, Governor Francis Fauquier, and Speaker Robinson for electing to build a new road through Pennsylvania to the confluence of the Ohio rather than follow the old Braddock path from the Potomac. Perhaps there were legitimate arguments for either approach, but it was the general's decision and not Washington's. He accused his superior of being hoodwinked by selfish Pennsylvanians panting to construct an artery that would enable them to corner the Ohio Valley trade at the expense of the Old Dominion. He encouraged Virginia officials to go over Forbes's head and even appeal directly to the king: "Let him know how grossly his Hon'r and the Publick money have been prostituted." Fortunately for Washington, Forbes proved to be a bigger man than the hotheaded colonel. He could still respect his adversary and employ him to good advantage, though stating sadly that "his Behaviour about the roads was no ways like a Soldier."[50]

In the last analysis, what can we say about George Washington in 1758, at the end of this first career in arms, beyond the very notable fact that he had encountered problems and controversies that would long constitute important features of the American military tradition? Highly educated at the war academy of hard knocks, he was a first-rate administrator and combat officer, a leader of men in action; he was tough, tenacious, brave, perhaps even inspirational. But a splendid field-grade officer does not always see his wartime role in broad perspective, nor is he usually required to. Much less is he likely to hold a colonelcy and to have such enormous responsibilities thrust upon him in his early-to-middle twenties. After all, he had not yet turned twenty-seven when he retired to Mount Vernon.

The irony mentioned previously refers to more than the realization that there were those who shed no tears over his departure from active duty—he who would one day rank among the great captains. The more significant irony is this: his most glaring weaknesses as a field-grade officer were to be corrected in time and were to become the sources of his greatest strength. His respect for and understanding of superior authority—that is to say, civil control of the military *and all that it meant*—became his most admirable soldierly quality in the War of Independence and his foremost contribution to the American military tradition.

TWO

Tradition in Transition

How do we explain his transformation? How did the twenty-six-year-old colonel of the Virginia Regiment, so hotheaded and critical of his superiors, obtain the breadth for which he is properly remembered today? Like any meaningful historical question, this one is assuredly complicated, and we can scarcely probe all its dimensions here. First, however, there is the simple element of maturity, which should offer in itself some benefits, as it appears to have done in Washington's case. His correspondence subsequently reveals a man less disposed to quick pronouncements and simplistic solutions, to placing his headaches at the doorstep of somebody else. Thank goodness Washington in 1775 was forty-three rather than twenty-six. Everything we know about him indicates that during those intervening seventeen years he became a more sober and judicious person.

The statement is not meant to imply that there was no mental growth on Washington's part between 1754 and 1758. In some respects he must have been a very different man as a result of his experiences during four stressful years as a military commander on the frontier. Not only were his accomplishments with the regiment impressive, but the final year also witnessed an improvement in his standing in the Virginia capital, both with the General Assembly and the new governor, the highly urbane Francis Fauquier. No doubt Washington by then had learned much, albeit slowly

and painfully, about dealing with his civilian lords. Unquestionably, too, the year 1758 was a less troublesome
time for the provincial commander because the tide of conflict had turned in favor of the Anglo-American side on the
Virginia-Pennsylvania frontier and because Pitt's generosity
in pounds and pence had substantially eased the financial
burdens of the Old Dominion.

A combination of these factors casts light on the quality
of his letters to Fauquier. When Washington did not have an
axe to grind, when he was not red under the collar about
this or that, he evinced not only a steadily improving prose
style but also the analytical tools essential for those who
themselves must make public decisions or influence the decision-making process. His missives are mostly judicious
and businesslike; they refer to options, alternatives, and
consequences respecting different military matters. There
is, finally, gracious praise for Forbes, the unfair victim of
Washington's anger over the Duquesne route some weeks
earlier. The general, "very assiduous" in consolidating his
hold on the area around the forks of the Ohio, had exhibited "great merit (which I hope will be rewarded) for the
happy issue he has brought our Affairs to."[1]

As for his broadening postwar experiences, Washington
undoubtedly sharpened his managerial skills, already evident as a colonial soldier, in successfully operating a large
Virginia plantation. His life at Mount Vernon was far different from that of a wealthy English country gentleman or an
indolent West Indian planter. He put in long hours closely
supervising the manifold activities of his estate. All those
endeavors, when combined with keeping business records,
allocating his financial resources, planning for the year
ahead as well as for the longer future, were doubtless responsibilities not wholly dissimilar to the management of
the Continental army in 1775. Alertness and enterprise, to

be sure, are needed equally in the worlds of business and soldiering.

We must give equal if not greater emphasis to Washington's decade and a half as a legislator, first in the Virginia House of Burgesses and then in the Continental Congress. From his burgess seat, beginning in 1759, he had to study such matters as taxation and expenditures as well as public policies from an angle of vision different from that of a soldier, to be conscious of electoral behavior and political realities—subjects often foreign to men in uniform. This study was good therapy for his impulsive tendencies. As a political newcomer, he observed and listened. He came to appreciate the deliberative process that characterized the conduct of legislative bodies—none more so than the Virginia house, which prided itself on its slow and judicious manner of conducting the public's business. Hasty and precipitate proposals, as freshman Patrick Henry discovered in 1765's Stamp Act debate, elicited a jaundiced eye from the senior circle of notables who had dominated the legislature for a generation or better, in this the oldest representative assembly in the New World.

The Continental Congress, to which Washington was elected in 1774, was a tribunal with certain characteristics quite unlike the stable and homogeneous House of Burgesses, which to a remarkable degree practiced the politics of consensus. If Congress too moved slowly, it did so not for the reasons that motivated the Virginia house but rather because the delegates at Philadelphia came from twelve, and eventually thirteen, colonies. They were men of diverse interests and backgrounds, somewhat jealous and suspicious of one another, sitting in an infant body which obviously lacked its own procedures and traditions. Pressured by a thousand and one concerns, particularly after the outbreak of hostilities at Lexington and Concord, it could

hardly be expected to manage its business in the atmosphere of the gentlemen's club that was the House of
Burgesses.

It is doubtful that Washington could have received better
training for his future role as commander in chief of the
Continental army. He had learned invaluable lessons in
Williamsburg and Philadelphia about the way political
bodies behaved and the legislative mind perceived matters.
He also became more sensitive to the nature and complexity
of the Anglo-American heritage of civil control of the military, a heritage scarcely present anywhere else in the eighteenth-century Western world; Britain herself seemed to
threaten this heritage after 1763 when for the first time, and
without consulting the provincial assemblies, a sizable
peacetime force was stationed permanently in North America. In this atmosphere Washington's French and Indian
War experience took on broader meaning for him. It did so
in the context of outpourings on such subjects as the evils of
maintaining standing armies free from the control of local
legislatures, the virtues of militias composed of upstanding
yeomen and artisans in place of long-term mercenaries, and
still other forms of civil-military friction. After all, who
among the congressmen at the Pennsylvania State House in
1775 had witnessed more civil-military altercations than
Washington and had actually been in the thick of them,
with both British regulars and Virginia civilian leaders as
his adversaries?

For these and still other reasons Washington was the best
qualified American for the highest military appointment.
His brief service as a division commander under Forbes had
given him the opportunity to lead a heavier body of troops
than any provincial officer who would become an American
general in the War of Independence. Even before then, he
had behaved with a strong element of military professionalism in training and leading his Virginia Regiment. In

this respect, too, he was unique among provincial officers during the French and Indian War.

Too much has been made of Washington's military limitations. Admittedly he lacked meaningful familiarity with artillery and cavalry, and he had never led a large army in open-field combat. Even his sympathetic biographer Douglas Freeman marvels at how unprepared he was for the formidable responsibilities thrust upon him, comparing the Virginian to a "mate on a merchantman . . . summoned overnight, as it were, to direct a convoy."[2] There are, however, no absolute criteria for predicting military attainments. Caesar and Cromwell, like Washington, were in their forties when they began their most serious soldiering. The duties of Grant and Lee as aides to Mexican War generals scarcely qualified them to direct hosts in the Civil War. Dwight Eisenhower, supreme allied commander in Europe during World War II, had never before seen combat in a career that extended back to 1915.

Congress, moreover, gave first priority to the political dimensions of military leadership in its choice. Had a lengthy professional career been their major criterion, the men at Philadelphia would undoubtedly have turned to Charles Lee or Horatio Gates, veteran British officers who had cast their lot with the patriot cause. On this score Washington was under no illusions. He recognized that Congress had voiced its full support of him primarily because its members knew and trusted him as a legislator, not as a soldier. They saw him as a fellow lawmaker who nonetheless knew more about the martial arts than they did, one who had been busily engaged the preceding year in reviving and training the Virginia militia and who had served on the various congressional committees dealing with preparations for defense in May and June of 1775. When the delegates described him to their constituents, they extolled his character and integrity; he was no longer the sometimes petulant, overly sensitive man with the uncontrollable ego of the 1750s. They also stressed, as he well knew, the value of appointing a Virginian as a way of drawing support from throughout the colonies for what had been until then mainly New England's war.[3]

From the day he accepted his commission from Congress, Washington showed abundant evidence of consciously employing his military and political background to good advantage. It is fortunate that he did. For the general and his army the period between July 1775 and March 1776—the months he conducted the siege of Boston—were to be the most crucial of the war. Part of the difficulty was that this marked his initial confrontation with the army he had once admired and longed to join. His counterpart—the first of four British commanding generals he outlasted in the course of the Revolution—was his once-warm friend of Monongahela days, Thomas Gage. This was the same Gage who had sympathized over Washington's failure to secure recognition and advancement, who in one missive had praised the young Virginian's "laudable Endeavours, & the Noble Spirits you have exerted in the Service of your Country."[4]

One wonders, as Washington looked out over Gage's forces in Boston, whether he reflected on those frustrated ambitions of yesteryear. Had he obtained a royal commission, how would the course of history have changed? The Continental army would have had a different commander in chief, and the Virginian would likely have dropped out of posterity's sight had he made for himself a permanent career wearing the king's colors. We can scarcely imagine that he would ever have become a general officer. Colonials in the British regular establishment simply did not advance to rarefied heights, lacking as they did the money to purchase expensive higher ranks and the close connections in London court circles that opened doors to preferment. Certainly those former times in arms remained vivid in his mind. July 3, 1775, the very day he assumed command of the Continental army encamped at Cambridge, was the twenty-first anniversary of his capitulation to the French at Fort Necessity; six days later marked an even two decades since Braddock's defeat. In July 1776, Washington reminded Adam Stephen, his old lieutenant colonel of the Virginia Regiment, that he "did not let the anniversary of the 3d or 9th . . . pass . . . without a grateful remembrance of the escape we had at the Meadows and on the Bank of Monongahela."[5]

If his first military career had begun with setbacks, would his second career in uniform also begin—and possibly end—in a defeat, one so devastating that it might result in the loss of his entire army and the collapse of the Revolution? While we know that he was keenly aware of that possibility, the eight-and-a-half months that he fronted Generals Gage and William Howe across Boston Neck were crucial for yet other reasons. They involved Washington's dealings with his own countrymen. Since he was given a rousing send-off by Congress and acclaimed by influential New England delegates, there has been a tendency in some quarters to minimize any worries about American civil-military relations in 1775. It can, of course, be said that the New England forces were raised in the towns in response to a particular danger and were enlisted only for the remainder of the year; they were therefore compatible with colonial military practices in the French and Indian War and consistent with American preferences for citizen soldiers.

Nevertheless, Massachusetts attitudes are not easy to simplify or untangle. Partly because of its inability to control effectively its own contingents, the Provincial Congress of the Bay colony had requested that the Continental Congress take charge of what had become known as the New

England Army of Observation. "We tremble," declared the Massachusetts body, "at having an Army (although consisting of our countrymen) established here, without a civil power to provide for and control them."[6] Could Washington, as the agent of the Continental Congress (that is, the "civil power"), exert authority over the army in such a manner as not to raise the hackles of the New Englanders, some of whom had preferred that Massachusetts's General Artemas Ward, an experienced warrior himself, be appointed commander in chief?

For years Massachusetts had complained of making excessive sacrifices in the cause of British America, and it had bridled at the heavy-handed use of British military power. "For over half of the period between 1689 and 1775," declares William Pencak, "Massachusetts mustered and taxed its inhabitants to a degree unduplicated in any other British colony." In the final conflict, she raised roughly six times the number of soldiers proportional to her white population as did Washington's Virginia. Governor Francis Bernard acknowledged that the province had suffered from the "severe taxation" it had imposed upon its citizens, "an immense sum for such a small state!"[7]

All available evidence bespeaks stronger suspicions and fears of armies and military regimentation in Massachusetts than elsewhere. Such fears were due in part to the colonists' Puritan heritage and their relationship to the radical whig intellectual tradition that had enormous impact on New England because of the close ties between religious dissenters on both sides of the Atlantic. Many of the anti-standing army writers in the mother country were Protestants of the left-wing variety, as were the New England Congregationalists. These concerns had heightened the civil-military disturbances between Massachusetts civilian authorities and provincial forces on the one hand and British officers on the other, conflicts as serious and prolonged as any colonial-British disputes. Pencak writes that "animosity against British officers and mismanaged expeditions marked the province's four great wars."[8]

There is further evidence to indicate that the Continental army began its existence in the colony most sensitive to the dangers of military intrusion, evidence at variance with the view that scant anti-redcoat feeling surfaced between the Treaty of Paris and the dispatch of scarlet regiments to Boston in 1768 during the Townshend crisis. Massachusetts, in fact, generated a good deal of literature between 1763 and 1768 in opposition to maintaining a regular establishment in America in time of peace.[9]

Moreover, when we add to this evidence the subsequent presence of redcoats and events such as the Boston Massacre and Gage's march to Concord, we can see that Washington needed to show great sensitivity to the people's concerns about armed forces in addition to handling his strictly military problems. After leaving Philadelphia with his commission in hand, he informed the New York and Massachusetts revolutionary assemblies that he had been motivated only by a sense of patriotism to relinquish "the enjoyments of domestic life" for a station he had not sought for himself. His "highest ambition" was to be "the happy instrument" of restoring "peace, liberty, and safety." Time and again throughout the war he labored to point out that there should be no gulf between the citizen and the soldier. As he explained to the New Yorkers, "When we assumed the Soldier, we did not lay aside the Citizen; and we shall most sincerely rejoice with you in that happy hour when the establishment of American Liberty, upon the most firm and solid foundations, shall enable us to return to our Private Stations in the bosom of a free, peaceful and happy Country."[10]

Washington's challenge was really severalfold. First, as the commander of an army that he hoped to fashion into an

effective military instrument, he had to contend with the
historic inabilities of the colonists to unite in the face of a
common danger. Save for the notable Louisbourg expedition of 1745, intercolonial military ventures had usually
been disastrous. Even if fortunate enough to be assembled,
coordinate provincial forces succumbed to discord, desertion, and disease. Washington had firsthand knowledge
of the inability of Virginia and her neighbors to execute
joint undertakings in the 1750s. The mature Washington
needed no reminder that the bickering between Virginia
and Pennsylvania over Forbes's route to Fort Duquesne had
seriously threatened the outcome of that campaign. And all
Americans knew the fate of Franklin's Plan of Union in
1754. Not a single British province had been willing to give
up its control of military affairs in favor of an intercolonial
tribunal. Washington might well have echoed Franklin's lament of that year: the "extreme difficulty of bringing so
many different governments and assemblies to agree in any
speedy and effectual measures for our common defense and
security, while our enemies have the very great advantage of
being under one direction, with one council and one
purse."[11]

To a considerable degree, the provincials conducting the
siege of Boston resembled an intercolonial force of the past.
Each of the four New England colonies had sent its own
separately organized army, over which there was no binding
central authority. The senior Massachusetts officers formed
a council of war, which ranking officers from Connecticut,
Rhode Island, and New Hampshire were invited to join.
However, it was scarcely a viable system for bringing order
out of what at times seemed chaos, as evidenced by the confusion on the patriot side during the Battle of Bunker Hill.

Could Washington meet his first challenge by bringing
about greater coordination than any provincial army had
ever attained? As a second challenge, could he also prevail

over what might be termed historic militia attitudes that ran
so counter to the discipline and organization he considered
essential? In short, could he overcome the obstacles that
had all but scuttled his efforts on the Virginia frontier two
decades before? Furthermore, could he accomplish this goal
at the very time when the militia was being glorified in the
American press and pulpit, depicted as the antithesis of and
also the antidote to Britain's professional army? To be sure,
the years 1774–1775 had witnessed a revival of the militia
up and down the Atlantic seaboard as provincial congresses
seized control from royal executives and made defense a
first priority. Institutionally, the militia in 1775 appeared to
be more formidable than at any time in memory. Its heroic,
if disorganized, performances at Concord and Bunker Hill
only served to reinforce the notion for many that it might
sustain America in the imperial crisis. Or as Thomas Jefferson boasted, Bunker Hill proved that a "want of discipline"
could be overcome "by native courage and . . . animation
in the cause." Still, the militia was the militia: a body of
uncoordinated irregulars from various colonies that could
not stand up to the British army in the long run.[12]

Washington's third challenge, equally rooted in colonial
warfare, was to avoid the kind of controversies that had be-
deviled relations between the British army and the colonists
in the French and Indian War, controversies involving impressment of supplies and equipment, quartering, recruitment, and treatment of militia and other locals in arms. For
Washington the shoe was on the other foot: he commanded
the regulars, the standing army; he therefore had no wish to
be involved in the seemingly incessant disputes that had
plagued the relations of Braddock and Loudoun with colonial assemblies.

Even Washington's early staunch advocate John Adams
was less than comfortable with the Continental army.
Adams cautioned William Tudor and James Warren that

armies must always be kept under strict civilian surveillance and that, consequently, he would be a "faithful
spy" on the army; Adams further urged that Tudor and
Warren should enlist in his espionage service. These sentiments are really not very surprising. Americans then and
now have been ambivalent about things military. Such sentiments are themselves a part of the complex, multidimen-
sional American military tradition. Adams and his cousin
Samuel maintained their ambivalence about Washington
and his army not only during its Cambridge encampment
but throughout the war as well; so did Elbridge Gerry, one
of the most influential members of the Massachusetts legislature in the fall of 1775. Though Gerry did his part to
maintain good relations between Washington and Massachusetts officials, he was unwilling to turn over full control of the colony's militia to Washington; Gerry believed
that provincial authorities should determine their numbers
and length of service when the commander in chief requested their assistance. Carrying the matter an additional
step was Samuel Adams, who felt that any time the militia
joined with the Continentals they should remain under the
absolute control of their own officers.[13]

It might be erroneous, however, to interpret the thinking
of Gerry and Adams as uncooperative or hostile. They may
well have sought to avoid friction not dissimilar to what the
province had experienced in past wars, especially with
Lord Loudoun in 1756, over the contractual nature of military participation. Loudoun had created a tempest by in-
sisting on taking charge of provincial troops raised in that
year for a campaign against the French at Crown Point and
Ticonderoga. Loudoun did so even though his predecessor
William Shirley had assured the New England officers and
men that theirs was an independent command, that they
would not be required to accept further assignments, and
that their enlistments were for only twelve months. To the

colonials' way of thought, Loudoun had no right to alter their terms of service. "Theirs was an argument especially resonant in New England," explains Fred Anderson; "a society fairly steeped in covenants: marriage covenants binding husbands and wives, church covenants among members of congregations, the great covenant of salvation between God and his chosen people. It did not, however, particularly resonate for Lord Loudoun."[14]

Washington, like Loudoun, was not directly familiar with New England, but he suffered no illusions about his formidable task. He responded to his challenges far more successfully than anyone familiar with the colonial military tradition had any right to predict. He combined his awareness of the need to be cautious and prudent with the knowledge that the Continental Congress had bestowed upon him broad discretion in the performance of his duties. He gave to the newborn army a structure and organization that would remain, with certain later modifications and reforms, throughout the war. He divided his command into brigades—usually six regiments in each—and his brigades into larger units designated as divisions. A centralized staff structure resulted from a series of appointments, some made by Washington, others by Congress; some positions closely resembling their counterparts in the British army, others more in line with the needs of a smaller force that could not rely for substantial assistance on a highly structured bureaucratic government like England's. In these undertakings he relied on British military practice, Congressional instructions, and the peculiar requirements of an American military establishment at that time.[15]

Washington also brought a good measure of order to the army, which was a frighteningly inept mass of humanity prior to his arrival in Cambridge. He may have remembered Gage's two-decades-old assertion to him that New Englanders were "the worst Soldiers on the Continent."

During the French and Indian War, General Phineas Lyman of Connecticut had conceded that the freedom and lack of restraint characteristic of New England society made it difficult for men to master the warrior's role. Initially Washington found substance in such remarks and said as much in several private letters, the contents of which became known in Philadelphia and caused him considerable embarrassment. Once his hand was called on the subject, he readily admitted his error; it did not result in irreparable injury to him. A sympathetic James Warren, president of the Massachusetts Provincial Congress, acknowledged that Washington had "many difficulties with officers and soldiers." Before long, however, the army showed vast improvement. Congress's articles of war, though neither so harsh as British military law nor so severe as Washington wished, helped bring order. Washington never waivered from his old conviction that discipline was the soul of any military organization. Contrary to radical whig theory, a citizen army might be as capable of misbehavior as the most dreaded European professional establishment. Without regulation, it might engage in acts that would offend the sensibilities and material welfare of the community.[16]

Although the soldiers doubtless thought Washington's methods stern if not draconian compared to the previous laxity of military life, the commander in chief gained the immediate support of the clergy, which had denounced the British army almost unanimously since the day of its appearance in Massachusetts in 1768. The clergy had claimed, as a contemporary historian phrased it, that the arrival of such an army "introduces a revolution in manners, corrupts the morals, propagates every species of vice, and degrades the human character." Such was not the case in Washington's army after he made his presence felt. "The regulations of the camp have been greatly for the better," reported the Reverend William Gordon, a frequent visitor.

"Before, there was little emulation among the officers: and the soldiers were lazy, disorderly, and dirty. The freedom to which the New Englanders have always been accustomed, makes them impatient of control [; but now] every officer and private begin to know his place and duty." Regimental Chaplain William Emerson, grandfather of Ralph Waldo Emerson, approved the "great overturning in the camp as to order and regularity. New lords, new laws." Now "great distinction is made between officers and soldiers. Everyone is made to know his place and keep it. . . . Thousands are at work every day from four till eleven o'clock in the morning. It is surprising how much work has been done."[17]

Washington was conscious from the outset of the war of what John Shy has termed the "triangularity" of the struggle, less a matter of two armies contending against each other as of two armed forces battling for the hearts and minds of America. Whether the complaint was that Continentals were bathing nude in a nearby river within eyesight of women of refinement or that they were tearing down fences and privies for firewood, Washington responded speedily to assuage civilian concerns. His general orders to the New England troops may well have sounded like the jeremiads that had descended on them in the past from meetinghouse pulpits; his stress on virtue, morality, and other behavior consistent with the ideals of the revolutionary cause were all of a piece with a protestant culture grounded in puritan values. One minister went so far as to proclaim the Continental army as the personification of piety and virtue.[18]

Consequently, the commander in chief could not put too much emphasis upon the "appearance" of the army—its behavior, health, and cleanliness. Indeed, he did all he could to minimize mixing between soldiers and civilians, since the presence of even the best-mannered forces posed inconveniences and hardships for the citizenry. At Cambridge, he

initially kept as many men as possible in tents until at least
some of them could be moved into newly constructed barracks in order to avoid the quartering controversies that had
plagued civil-military relations in the French and Indian
War. For several reasons, including his wish to avoid intrusion on the civilian sector, Washington normally quartered
his army in the countryside and away from urban centers
throughout the war. According to Nathanael Greene, he
feared that troops cooped up in camp would "run mad with
pleasure" if exposed to city life and engage in "diversions of
all kinds." The same attitude governed his thinking while on
the march. On the way south to oppose Sir William Howe in
1777, for example, he hustled the more disreputable portion
of his long procession around Philadelphia so as not to offend
the Quakers.[19]

Finally, when we turn to Washington's third challenge,
we find that he avoided serious confrontations with both the
Continental Congress and the colonial governments in the
Northeast. He assuredly felt numerous irritants, most of
them stemming from political matters. The revolutionary
governments simply refused to sanction a consolidated
army that swept away local distinctions and concerns. He
was displeased that Congress found it necessary to allow
the various regiments to maintain their old designations because Massachusetts men did not want Rhode Islanders
serving in their regiments, Connecticut men did not wish
New Hampshirites, and so on. Then, too, the colonies con-
trolled the appointment and promotion of offices through
the rank of colonel, a practice diametrically opposed to his
thinking and experience. Washington had won from Governor Dinwiddie the authority to make most of the officer appointments for the Virginia Regiment. He had argued that
such authority was "of the utmost consequence" since,
among other things, "a Commanding Officer is answerable
for the behavior of the inferior Offices." Even so, the Phila-

delphia lawmakers persisted in elevating officers through
their own state lines. Rather than, for instance, choosing a
talented, experienced Pennsylvanian to head a New Jersey
regiment, they selected the Jersey man who ranked highest
on the state's seniority list, regardless of his ability.[20]

Likewise, Congress's choice of most generals in 1775
emitted a strong political aroma, as of course did its selection of Washington as commander in chief. New England,
which so far had supplied the troops, received two of the
four major generals and most of the brigadiers. Subsequently, state jealousies also led Congress to desire an equi-
table ratio between the number of general officers from a
state and that state's overall manpower contribution to the
army. In this context Benedict Arnold suffered a humilia-
tion from which he never recovered. Though probably the
army's most effective combat officer, he was denied a promotion to major general in February 1777, primarily because his home state of Connecticut already had two generals of that rank. Congress proceeded to elevate to major
general five officers clearly lacking Arnold's ability. Equally
inferior to Arnold was one of Connecticut's major generals,
Israel Putnam, who was popular in his own colony and was
also the only general officer, save for Washington, to be
elected unanimously by Congress. Putnam's mistakes at
Long Island and in the Hudson Highlands made him a burden for Washington that was only lifted when "Old Put"
suffered a career-ending stroke in 1779. Of sixty-four-year-
old Major General Joseph Frye of Massachusetts, Washington wrote: "I doubt he will . . . do much service to the
cause; at present he keeps to his room, and talks learnedly
of emetics, cathartics, &c. For my own part, I see nothing
but a declining life that matters him." Happily for all concerned, Frye held his commission for only a month before
resigning for reasons of health.[21]

Anger and resentment over promotion issues, which agitated the Continental army from beginning to end, have never ceased to disturb the American military establishment. The nineteenth century witnessed political generals in all American wars, a price that civilian executives and military commanders had to pay in order to appease influential sectors of the home front. During the Civil War, General U. S. Grant—like Washington before him—achieved some of his greatness because of his ability to endure subordinates like Benjamin F. Butler who were as incompetent as they were untouchable.

Notwithstanding his preference for military proficiency, Washington might have suffered equally or more had he gained control of all promotions, since strong jealousies marked intercolonial relations. A merit system can produce still other kinds of difficulties, as Americans discovered when seniority practices gave way—in theory at any rate—to merit considerations near the end of the nineteenth century. At least Washington did not have to face from within the office cadre the charge of favoritism regarding rank, as did the leaders responsible in this century for leaping John J. Pershing over 862 senior officers. Pershing's case is comparable to the meteoric rise of Alexander Haig, "the most blatant military political appointee in over half a century," according to Richard K. Betts, who reminds us that Haig rose from lieutenant colonel to four-star general in under five years.[22] Even had congress and the states conceded to Washington authority over all promotions, he would have been perpetually in hot water with Congress, or the states, or the army—or all three!

As it was, Washington had to sidestep the promotion issue on one occasion in 1775 that did involve all three. When General John Thomas of Massachusetts and his military admirers became upset because another Bay colony officer received a higher seniority ranking than Thomas, and when the Massachusetts legislature sided with Thomas and urged the commander in chief to re-rank him, Washington may have seen that dispensing promotions could be a two-edged sword. He prudently placed the delicate matter before the Continental Congress, where it properly belonged.[23]

On another matter concerning the generals, Washington set the policy and subsequently received congressional backing. In so doing he gave the American military tradition a push toward democracy, although at the time he described his policy as a way to avoid favoritism and jealousy, already too prevalent among the New Englanders. He terminated the practice of permitting a general officer to command one of his provincial regiments. Besides the fact that they would incur the resentment of other generals who lacked a regimental command, senior commanders were sufficiently busy with their more encompassing duties. Washington also realized that they would be vulnerable to charges of partiality toward their individual regiments. There was something akin to a feeling of ownership on the part of some generals, exemplified by Massachusetts's William Heath, who claimed the right of designating his successor if he gave up his unit. Such a sense of possession was a reality in the British army, where a regiment was a sinecure carrying rewards without responsibilities, where generals and colonels headed regiments without being directly in control of them; they profited handsomely and normally delegated regular leadership duties to lieutenant colonels.[24]

At no time was serious consideration given to a further aspect of the royal military system: allowing officers to buy and sell their commissions. Washington was painfully familiar with this practice from his failing endeavors to obtain crimson regimentals in the 1750s. We do know that some Continental officers favored adopting the purchase system. One uniquely American argument of proponents was that an officer who had a financial stake in his unit's reputation would work harder than otherwise to improve its proficiency. But such a system had no chance of ever securing the approval of Washington or Congress. The image of British officers as worldly, selfish, and dissolute—an image fostered by colonial anti-army literature—was not of a piece with American cultural values and the principles of the Revolution.

As the war lengthened, Continental officers were to feel the sting of criticism from various quarters; they were charged, for example, with seeing themselves as a class or caste apart from their fellow revolutionists. Indeed, that particular complaint against the officer corps continued to dog the army throughout the nineteenth century, sometimes in the context of debates over the United States Military Academy. Was West Point an institution of special privilege in a republic? In any event, it could never be said that top-ranking American officers held regimental benefices and that commissions might go to the highest bidder. Nor, for that matter, could it be demonstrated that officership— then or in later wars—was the preserve of the highest social orders, somehow comparable to a depraved European aristocracy. Washington himself wanted more, not fewer, gentlemen officers, because he believed (rightly or wrongly) that they nourished leadership qualities not found in the middling social elements; he never got them from a society that was fluid and legally unstructured.[25]

An endless string of issues had the potential to derail Washington in the opening phase of his undertaking. The next one involved the composition of the army's rank and file, an issue that has not lost its divisive nature over the past two hundred years. The size of military forces, their professional as opposed to amateur status, and their relationship to the citizenry (should the army be a cross-section of society?) are questions that have had enduring implications for the welfare of the American people and their public institutions.

Washington's views on these matters have been oversimplified. While we have addressed his criticism of colonial militia, it is his remarks about militia in the Revolution that have been quoted from his day to ours. Advocates of a substantial professional military establishment in peacetime argued that it would spare the nation from being unprepared at the onset of a grave crisis and would therefore avoid an experience like Washington's in 1775. In his initial letter to Congress after taking command of the army, Washington made the first of his oft-quoted statements, declaring "that no Dependence can be put on the Militia for a continuance in Camp, or Regularity and Discipline during the short time they may stay."[26]

Even so, Washington never castigated the local military organizations as did some of his Continental officers. He saw separate but mutually supportive functions for Continentals and militia. Since the main army could not be everywhere, could not in particular defend the colonies against their internal enemies (the war-weary, the loyalists, and Indians), he believed that internal security must be the responsibility of the state constabularies. In emergencies militia should be pressed into service with the main army to play a supporting role, although they should never be considered an adequate substitute for Continentals.[27]

Yet Washington did not launch his tenure as commander in chief by badgering Congress for a long-term army that would remind his countrymen of a European professional establishment, one at odds with their character and traditions. It is never easy to wage war in a manner consistent with the ideals of a free people, which included for Americans the belief that citizens performing through their militias should have an equal share in society's military responsibilities. Washington was painfully aware of his dilemma between the ideal and the real—he who had been disappointed that so few of his fellow Virginians in the 1750s had come forth to fight, and then only because of coercive measures or special inducements. Now in the fall of 1775, as he contemplated how to plan for the following year, he found that a high percentage of his soldiers were unwilling to sign up for 1776. The discipline and training that he had taught the army in 1775 would in large part have to be repeated in 1776, since thousands of men were needed to replace those who failed to reenlist.

However tempted, Washington did not threaten or coerce the soldiers into giving him extra weeks to carry the army through its manpower crisis. That would have provoked their provincial governments, let alone the rank and file. (Past wars had witnessed the mutiny of New England troops because they were being detained beyond the expiration of their terms or because they feared they would be restrained from returning home.) Conscious of having honored their contractual obligations to their respective colonies and to the Continental army, hundreds, eventually thousands, drifted away, just as their fathers and forefathers had done in bygone campaigns, as Washington watched helplessly. William Gordon was only one of a number of observers from the region who attributed their behavior to a peculiar New England "cast" of mind. Governor Jonathan Trumbull of Connecticut, in saying much the same thing, did not attempt to defend them—troops from his own colony were the first to leave. Contractual thinking was, for better or worse, taken literally; it was "the genius and spirit of our people," reflected as fully "in the last war" as in 1775.[28]

Some historians have faulted Washington for his anger at their behavior and for his failure to understand their values and way of thinking. As his reenlistment headaches mounted, he privately railed at "the dearth of public spirit, and want of virtue" within the army; "such a dirty, mercenary spirit pervades the whole, that I should not be at all surprised at any disaster that may happen."[29] But it is more important to stress that he only verbalized his frustrations, that he did not overreact by breaking faith with the mustering-out men. Careful not to antagonize local officials, he urged the colonies to draft auxiliaries to meet the emergency. His restraint reaped rewards. New England's political and military leaders, chagrined over feeble reenlistments, did turn out their militias promptly and in numbers that amazed Washington, who had only unhappy memories of militia mobilizations in Virginia.[30]

Already by the year's end he seems to have been thinking beyond the new one-year army being recruited for 1776. In the previous fall he had deliberately shied away from urging the use of bounties to obtain enlistments, a step favored by some New England delegates but opposed in late 1775 by most members of the Continental Congress. Slowly the commander in chief moved toward openly espousing the controversial and closely related ideas of bounties and long enlistments. His first letter to lawmakers on the subject was not penned until February 1776, three weeks after such a proposal had been introduced and defeated in that body and well after his initial trials of raising a new one-year army. All the same, he recommended the two measures with some trepidation. After all, he realized his countrymen's historic aversion to "standing armies" and doubtless knew the fate of the previous month's resolution. He "ask[ed] pardon for intruding an opinion, not only unasked, but in some measure repugnant." For reasons of economy, efficiency, and effectiveness he could see no alternative to paying men bounties to enlist for the duration of the war. "To expect the same Service from Raw, and undisciplined Recruits as from Veteran Soldiers, is to expect what never did, and perhaps never will happen," he warned. Even if men enlisted in greater numbers for a single year, which was not occurring for the second year of the war (1776), it defied all logic to have an old army go and a new army arrive each year "within musket shot of the Enemy," as Washington had earlier expressed it. Surely "it is not in the pages of History . . . to furnish a case like ours."[31]

Not unexpectedly, Congress's decision was slow in coming.[32] Still, the spring and summer brought a discernible trend toward Washington's position. Some Continentals were enlisted for two or more years, and in some cases financial inducements were extended to those signing up for three years. In September, Congress went the full distance, resolving to offer cash bounties and land grants in the hope of raising over sixty thousand men for the duration of hostilities.

Washington's tactful advocacy was crucial to the outcome, although he received some unanticipated support in Congress because of the dismal news from the secondary American field army, commanded by General Philip Schuyler. The New Yorker's invasion of Canada had met with failure partly because his troops had departed almost en masse after enlistments expired at year's end. Further aid came from New England congressmen John and Samuel Adams, who were normally outspoken critics of standing armies and had voted against the original motion for a regular army in 1776. The like-minded Elbridge Gerry, newly elected to Congress, joined with them.[33]

Actually, the commander in chief strengthened Congress's authority at every turn, deferring to it on important and sometimes trivial questions and informing New England leaders who bombarded him with requests that their entreaties should be submitted to the lawmakers in Philadelphia. At the same time, he politely but firmly made it clear that he held his commission from Congress and therefore was not subject to the directives of any colony or state government. Strange as it may seem, given the historic jealousies and localism that had always hampered intercolonial relations, Washington successfully denied the military jurisdiction of colonial or state governments, as well as their requests for Continental troops for their immediate defense. With equal success he persuaded them to forward from their own resources supplies and equipment for his army, at the same time that he carefully respected their political jurisdiction and control over the militia.[34] Thus, he seems to have been as conscious of setting vital precedents in the opening round of the war as he was upon assuming the presidency many years later. In 1775, however, he thought only of precedents for a war; he was not then aware that in less than a year the war would become a struggle for American independence and that his wartime precedents would become lasting precedents for civil-military relations in America. The temptation on the part of local and regional politicians to meddle in military operations did not halt immediately; there were instances of such efforts at interference in other military theaters in the Revolution and occasionally in the future—for instance, during the postwar Confederation years and during the War of 1812. For the most part, however, the supremacy of the central government in military affairs has been maintained since Washington's day.

Nonetheless, precedents become lasting less because of their proximity to legality than because of the respect accorded to the civilian or military leader in question. So it was with Washington. If he arrived in Massachusetts with a healthy measure of respect, he added to it. Washington sensed from the outset that he was a diplomat in a coalition war involving a weak extralegal central government in the form of Congress and thirteen regional governments stretching from New Hampshire to Georgia. In all forms of diplomacy, military or otherwise, direct communication is imperative. During the nine months that he was headquartered at Cambridge, he wrote fifty-one letters to the president of Congress, thirty-four to the Massachusetts legislature, forty to Governor Jonathan Trumbull of Connecticut, and thirty to Governor Nicholas Cooke of Rhode Island.[35] In doing so he kept civilian leaders abreast of his plans and needs and of enemy activities. While there may have been occasional disappointments and disagreements, there were no communication barriers of the kind that strained relations between President James K. Polk and General Winfield Scott in the Mexican War and between President Abraham Lincoln and General George B. McClellan in the Civil War.

The British departure from Boston gave Washington additional months to prepare for the confrontation that still lay in the future. The king's ministers were scarcely ready to mount an offensive that might bring the colonies to their knees. That awareness, together with Washington's fortification of heights overlooking the Massachusetts capital, explains why General William Howe, Gage's replacement, sailed away on March 17, 1776, and subsequently combined his command with an invasionary armada from the parent kingdom. Our textbooks and strong defense proponents continue to remind us that America has begun its wars in a state of unpreparedness from the time of the Revolution, if not before. The same usually held true for the nation's adversaries as well, prior to the conflicts of the twentieth century. The London government had to raise and transport numerous forces, which needed training.

It is a commonplace that British detachments in overseas garrisons were invariably in poor condition; it has also been assumed that troops in Britain and Ireland were in far better shape at the outset of foreign wars. An investigation of inspection returns and marching orders for the eighteenth-century army exposes the fallacy of that notion. Divided and dispersed, home regiments were almost always on the go—preoccupied with domestic functions, maintaining law and order as a kind of police force and working alongside customs officials, patrolling the shoreline in the never-ending surveillance against smugglers. Only in Ireland were there adequate barracks. The result was that soldiers elsewhere were boarded in small groups in villages and towns, often at great inconvenience to the local folk.[36]

Under these circumstances peacetime training was sporadic at best, even at the company level. In battalions it occurred only once a year for ten days, in order to ready the men for the annual inspection—the only occasion when they could expect to be viewed by general officers. (The latter devoted themselves almost entirely to social pursuits between wars.) Joint training for more than one battalion was virtually unknown, declares Piers Mackesy, who adds that "there were no permanent camps in Great Britain with room enough for a brigade exercise." Hard, intensive exercises could only take place in wartime.[37] In the eighteenth century that usually meant on the European continent or in the New World rather than in Great Britain itself. The British people, obviously hostile to redcoats crowded upon them, were spared most of the trouble connected with heavy concentrations of forces. Yet Americans in the War of Independence would feel the impact of two contending armies. The presence of even a single army, though composed of Washington's Continentals, would scarcely be a positive experience.

Washington had inherited an army that seemed huge, unprecedented in size by colonial standards. Whereas three thousand provincials had joined in the capture of Louisbourg in 1745 and nearly five thousand had assembled in the Albany-Schenectady staging area for strikes at French bases to the north and west in 1755, Washington's strength returns show an army (on paper at least) of over twenty-three thousand men at its high point in the fall of 1775.[38] It was spread in an arc around the land side of Boston, stretching from the Mystic River on the north to Dorchester on the south. (That region, teeming with villages and farmsteads, had not only the Continental army to disrupt its normal life but also streams of refugees from British-occupied Boston. By August 1775, 6,753 civilians out of a prewar population of sixteen thousand remained in what had once been "the metropolis of North America.")[39]

When Washington first arrived, he learned that many civilians felt at the mercy of an uncontrolled army. Groups of provincial soldiers wandered from town to town and from house to house begging for necessities; many had lost or left clothes and bedding in their hasty retreat from Bunker Hill.

How different was the view of Washington's army the following year as it prepared to leave Massachusetts in anticipation of Howe's attacking New York! The commander in chief's demonstrable concern for the public welfare contrasted sharply with what Massachusetts's own militia generals had been able to accomplish before his arrival. His record also stood out in bold relief as opposed to the behavior of the army of Gage and Howe. Bay colony leaders found Boston left in deplorable condition. Over two hundred houses as well as Old North Church had provided firewood for its royal garrison as four generations of ministers named Mather must have moaned in their graves. Fuel demands also cost Jonathan Mayhew's West Church its steeple. At Old South, pews were torn out and the floor covered with gravel to make a riding school for royal horsemen. "Despite strict orders," says G. B. Warden, the departing redcoats "plundered every unprotected shop and house in town."[40]

For all their reservations in principle about standing armies, New Englanders believed that George Washington, a Virginian, had earned their trust with what was a potentially dangerous military instrument. It was obvious to all but the most suspicious and doctrinaire souls that Washington and his army had given no evidence of threatening American liberties. Though still untested in battle, he had been examined in other important respects and earned the highest marks from those most able to judge his record: the Massachusetts revolutionary government and the Continental Congress. While both bodies praised him for his character and for his success in securing the freedom of Boston, two further tributes from the Massachusetts representatives are significant for a developing American military tradition. The New Englanders felt that he had displayed just the right touch in administering an army composed of Americans: he had been "mild, yet strict" in his "government of the army." If he had been demanding and stern when necessary, he had nonetheless treated their sons and neighbors as free men rather than as European mercenaries. He had, in addition, paid strict "attention to the civil constitution of this colony." The latter, even more than the former, was an incredible accomplishment in the morning of a war and a revolution.[41]

Repeating their words in his reply, Washington expressed particular appreciation for their recognition of his "attention to the civil constitution." He carried his acknowledgment a step farther: "A regard to *every* Provincial institution, where not incompatible with the common interest, I hold a principle of duty and policy, and it shall ever form a part of my conduct."[42] Nor was there any Caesar-like behavior about the liberation of the provincial capital or any triumphant entry by the commander in chief, who instead of riding at the head of his advance regiments attended divine services at the meeting house in Cambridge.

Because the Continental Congress had found its initial trust in Washington not only confirmed but strengthened, the delegates were more willing to risk the uncertainties of declaring their independence from Great Britian in the summer of 1776. Had he acted in a high-handed, arbitrary manner, reviving memories of a Loudoun in the 1750s or a Gage of more recent years, these delegates would have been less willing to put a large measure of their fate in the hands of the commander in chief of their forces. After all, why cast off a king and his army only to be threatened by a general leading an army of their own countrymen?

THREE

The Revolutionary Tradition

WASHINGTON WAS UNDERSTANDABLY IN A REFLECTIVE MOOD as the first phase of the war ended and he girded his loins for the next round. To his brother John Augustine he summarized his feelings: "I believe I may, with great truth affirm, that no Man perhaps since the first Institution of Armys ever commanded one under more difficult Circumstances, than I have done. To enumerate the particulars would fill a volume." Withal, he was delighted "to hear from different Quarters, that my reputation stands fair, that my Conduct hitherto has given universal Satisfaction. The Addresses which I have received, and which I suppose will be published, from the General Court [legislature] of this Colony . . . and from the Selectmen of Boston upon the evacuation of the Town and my approaching departure from the Colony, exhibits a pleasing testimony of their approbation of my conduct, and of their personal regard, which I have found in various other Instances; and which, in retirement, will afford many comfortable reflections."[1]

With independence, however, came new problems, which necessitated that Washington call upon the reservoir of good will he had skillfully built up during the first year of conflict. Beginning in the summer of 1776, after moving from Boston to New York, his Continentals became a fighting army. Historically, American armies in wartime have steadily improved in their overall combat performance. If the Vietnam conflict may be an exception to this generalization,

it is unquestionably valid for the Revolution, particularly
for the main army under Washington's immediate command. Still, the divisions under the Virginian's direct jurisdiction did not perform consistently well until 1778.

Most of all, in an eight-and-a-half-year military struggle
(twice the length of the Civil War or of World War II), the
Continental army needed staying power, the ability to survive. It had to be an object of concern to British commanders, a source of intimidation for the loyalists, a rallying
point for the militia, and a living, day-to-day symbol of the
Revolution and of emerging American nationality. The
point about survival is worth underscoring, since historians
in the last generation have raised serious doubts whether
Britain ever had a good opportunity to achieve a clear-cut
military triumph. They have questioned whether the Revolution was not such an unprecedented struggle in terms of
its arduous demands in logistics, strategy, communication,
and coordination as to all but exclude that possibility.[2]

But if to exist was almost to insure against British victory,
how easy was it for Washington to survive? For one thing, as
we shall see, the Continental army was never numerically
more than a shadow of the more than sixty-thousand-man
force that Congress had agreed to raise for the duration in
1776. Small though it always was by the standard of European armies, it nevertheless needed more supplies and
equipment than Congress and the states seemed able to de-
liver. These developments, as well as other problems not
fully anticipated during the Boston siege, brewed serious
civil-military tensions.

Let us elaborate on these observations, first by looking at
Washington's dealings with the army and then by examin-
ing his relations with Congress over the long haul. There
was a good deal in his field-grade experience of the French
and Indian War that proved valuable to him as a commanding general. Like the colonel of the Virginia Regiment, Gen-

eral Washington considered himself a teacher, not only in his general orders directed principally at the rank and file (whom he had rarely tried to reach directly during his first military career) but also in his specific instructions to his officers. It was almost as though Washington had issued to the Continental officers the same wisdom, with some emendations, that he had imparted to his subordinates on the frontier of the Old Dominion. Washington had advised his provincial subordinates that "actions, and not the commission . . . make the Officer . . . there is more expected from him than the *Title*." In 1775 he elaborated on the same advice: "When Officers set good Examples it may be expected that the Men will with zeal and alacrity follow them, but it would be a mere phenomenon in nature, to find a well disciplin'd Soldiery where Officers are relax'd and tardy in their duty; nor can they with any kind of propriety, or good Conscience, set in Judgment upon a Soldier for disobeying an order, which they themselves are everyday breaking."[3]

Since he continued with the Revolutionary army to show the ability to win and hold the respect of men who served under him, there has been a tendency to term Washington a charismatic figure. In some respects he was, though he had none of the flamboyance or stem-winding oratorical style of Patrick Henry, Theodore Roosevelt, or Huey Long. His charisma was partly owing to his position as the military leader of a revolution; furthermore, standing six feet tall or better, he resembled the leader he was. Abigail Adams remarked that he looked more like a king than did George III.

One cannot trade exclusively on imposing looks or other charismatic qualities indefinitely, however, and in truth some contemporaries described Washington as reserved and aloof; a few less charitable souls saw a royal hauteur or sniffed an aroma of arrogance about him. Can we square such characterizations of Washington in his forties and fifties with the young colonel who stimulated feelings of warmth

and affection from his subordinates? At least we can say that
the general was older and operating on a wider stage with
broader responsibilities, not within the familiar confines of
the Virginia gentry from which he and his militia officers had
come nearly two decades earlier. Even so, he was always far
more comfortable around his army than in the performance
of his presidential duties, when he was often on public dis-
play. Whatever its origins, there was a distant side to Washington. He realized it himself, and he exercised it in a cal-
culating manner to reinforce his image as one who eschewed
pettiness, favoritism, and partisanship. His reserve gave him
added authority because it elicited greater respect, enabling
him to exact dutiful performance as rigorously from others as
from himself. If Washington failed to coin the saying that
"familiarity breeds contempt," he should have; the person
who coined it should have had him in mind.

Somehow he managed to keep his distance from men as
individuals, to avoid intimate relationships, and yet to convey—as he had to his Virginians in the 1750s—a spirit of
togetherness, endeavoring "to harmonize so many discor-
dant parts."[4] The officers' bond of shared experiences became so strong that in 1783 Steuben and Knox took the
lead in forming the Society of the Cincinnati, whose purpose was "to perpetuate" their memories and relationships
"as long as they shall endure, or any of their male posterity." Of course, it is easier to create esprit de corps in an
army than in most other human organizations. In Washington's case, however, the job was infinitely harder than
usual. He had to create a new army without shared traditions and composed of men almost exclusively from civilian
backgrounds from all over America—frontier to seaboard,
New Hampshire to Georgia. These men initially did not
even think of themselves as Americans but rather as Virginians, or Pennsylvanians, or Marylanders. It was just as well
that a host of the more parochial and selfishly motivated

officers had left the service by 1778. They had been soured by the influence of foreign officers, denial of promotion, and lack of salary and retirement remunerations. The generally high quality of the officer corps from the middle of the war onward was extremely important in light of Congress's inability to recruit the large army that was projected in 1776, for the officer complement confronted the endless task of training fresh recruits. Instead of recruiting solely for the duration of the war, as the 1776 act stipulated, the lawmakers soon accepted three-year enlistments and short-term men who were either drafted or recruited by the states for several months to a year.

At war's end, Washington, doubtless pushing to the back of his mind the agonies of officers' conflicts and empty regiments, wrote that no one would have imagined "that Men who came from the different parts of the Continent, strongly disposed, by the habits of education, to despise and quarrel with each other, would instantly become one patriotic band of brothers."[5] If he exaggerated the suddenness of the transformation of a motley colonial force into a national army, he also modestly ignored his guiding hand in the process.

How was it accomplished? First, his own example was crucial. Not only did he accept no pay for his services (only for his expenses, which he meticulously kept), but he also served for eight-and-a-half years without a leave of absence. Of course, deeds as well as example are essential aspects of military leadership, and they involve risks both on and off the battlefield. Never one to confine his tactics to the tent or the drawingboard to be carried out by subordinates, Washington was close to the action in every one of his battles; not infrequently he was in the thick of things, seemingly addicted to the smell of gunsmoke in his nostrils. The middle-aged General Washington, like Colonel Washington, was still brave, sometimes foolishly so, but his undaunted cour-

age was inspirational at Harlem Heights, Princeton, Mon-
mouth, and elsewhere. Officers' accounts of Washington's
personal courage are consistent with testimonials from enlisted men. Some appear in diaries and others in pension
statements filed decades afterward, a kind of documenta-
tion only just now receiving careful attention. While any
one of these recollections might be a questionable source,
collectively they convey a picture of Washington on the battlefield at one with declarations made at the time.

No general can be in all places at the same time or know
all that goes on. Nor should senior officers recklessly expose
themselves as Washington sometimes did. Yet the general
cannot forget his field-grade experience. Somehow he has to
impress upon men at all levels the fact that he is in control
and on top of things. Sergeant Joseph Plumb Martin, the
only man with the Sappers and Miners at Yorktown to pen
his memoirs, recalled that when the Americans were ready
to dig the first parallel, Washington himself "struck a few
blows with a pickax, a mere ceremony, so that it might be
said that 'General Washington with his own hands broke
ground at the siege of Yorktown.'" After the ninety-two
French and American cannon were in place along the opening parallel, it was Washington once again who ignited the
first weapon, which was followed by a "furious" discharge
up and down the line. Fortunately for Washington, he was
born before armies and business organizations were af-
flicted by overdoses of red tape and chains of command.[6]

Quite obviously, Washington got the message across not
only by exemplifying battlefield bravery but also by revealing a real flair for the dramatic—this same man who has
sometimes been dubbed a dullard and a solemn old bore.
He sensed as a soldier when to show the kind of emotion
that all men feel at times but that some, including Washington, find so difficult to reveal. (This is the same man,
who turned beet red, stammered, and avoided eye contact

with his audience when delivering his presidential inaugural address in 1789.) This flair for the dramatic—we might call it a keen mastery of psychology—he used with superb effect when he appeared before each regiment of the Continental army on December 30, 1776, just as many of their enlistments expired. He appealed to the soldiers to stay on for another six weeks as a special favor to him and to their country, so that what became known as the Trenton-Princeton campaign might be pressed to a glorious conclusion. It was a day when he won over two-thirds of the soldiers scheduled for departure, a day they never forgot. John C. Dann, who has examined hundreds of Revolutionary pension narratives, says that untold numbers recorded that they had continued in the service as a personal tribute to General Washington.[7] Though remembered now as a tough disciplinarian, Washington's soldiers thought of him as a kindhearted commander; indeed he may have been particularly tender to young men, possibly because he had no sons of his own.

It was well for him that he was so well regarded, for eighteenth-century battles were characterized more by manpower than by firepower. Men rather than machines of destruction ruled the day. Consequently, personal leadership at all levels was vitally important. Aging veterans boasted of having fought with General Washington, just as their grandsons would brag of riding with "Stonewall" or being alongside Lee at Gettysburg or Grant at Vicksburg. The impersonality of twentieth-century conflict is brought home when veterans speak of serving with a division or headquarters unit.

As for risks off the battlefield, they too took nerve on his part. For instance, given the degree of hostility in the army toward foreign officers by the time of the Valley Forge encampment, Washington initially may well have shown real courage in relying so heavily upon the Prussian veteran,

Frederich Wilhelm von Steuben, who arrived at the commander in chief's headquarters as a volunteer still without an American commission. Washington entrusted to the former major under Frederick the Great the formidable assignment of establishing a uniform system of drill and sought his advice on major administrative matters as well, all with splendid results. Washington eventually successfully nominated the German to be inspector general of the army. Nor was Washington reluctant to rely in the corps of engineers on able, experienced Frenchmen, particularly Brigadier General Louis Duportail and the French-trained Pole, Colonel Thaddeus Kosciuszko.[8]

Already Washington was showing a characteristic of outstanding leadership usually associated solely with his presidency, when his cabinet included Thomas Jefferson and Alexander Hamilton. It was the characteristic of placing around him in key positions men of outstanding ability who possessed some talents greater than his own—men from whom he could learn and consequently profit in the performance of his duties. Washington was always a good listener; during the war he spent hundreds of nights around the fireside in conversation with his native American officers and European soldiers who brought with them their Old World experiences. Though no backslapper, he made it a habit through dinners and in still other ways to make himself accessible to subordinates—a trait lacking in Lord Wellington and General Douglas MacArthur, two other aloof warrior chieftains. All the same Washington was his own man, no more dominated by the Rhode Islander Nathanael Greene as commander in chief than dwarfed by Alexander Hamilton as president. Washington found councils of war useful for the same reason that he created the cabinet as chief executive; through both bodies he could hear a mixture of opinions before making *his* decision. Admittedly, Congress instructed Washington to hold councils of war, an established military practice, but there is every reason to believe that he would have held them anyway. In the absence of direct evidence, one may even guess that Washington borrowed his ideas on the subject of war councils from General James Forbes, who had skillfully endeavored to elicit different views from his British and provincial officers and then had sought to create a consensus after a full airing of all opinions. To be thoughtful and reflective, to be sensitive to the complexity of vital matters, to go so far as to request opinions in writing well before councils of war or cabinet meetings—all this in the view of some critics then and now conveyed weakness, whereas in reality it showed good judgment. The proof is in the overall record of the general and president.

Just as he surrounded himself with obviously able men, so too he brought out the best in others who served under him, individuals who moved from obscurity to play prominent parts in the war. They made every effort to measure up to his expectations. Staff officers felt a keen personal obligation to the commander in chief. One historian writes that the much-berated supply officers not only admired but actually loved Washington, whose table they kept well-stocked whenever possible. To incur the general's displeasure, moaned Deputy Commissary Ephraim Blaine, was to make him "the most unhappy Man living." Or as another phrased it, he would do anything to keep the approval of "the best Man in the World."[9] Not surprisingly, the Virginian's aides shared these sentiments. These young officers chosen to be a part of his "military family" (especially Alexander Hamilton and John Laurens) not only were intelligent but also grew in maturity and understanding of the complex problems involved in completing a revolution and creating a nation. Speaking of Washington, Laurens assured his father Henry that "if ever there was a man in the world . . . fitted . . . for the command of a re-

publican army, he is, and he merits an unrestrained
confidence."[10]

Washington, a practical man rather than a creative
thinker, never wrote a military treatise, but for that matter
we do not find in the Revolution any truly original American contribution to organized professional warfare. There
were no military writers on the patriot side to compare with
the political writings of the Jeffersons and Adamses. Yet
Washington was mindful that the most innovative military
literature after mid-century came from France; he encouraged his officers to familiarize themselves with the latest
Gallic authors, just as earlier in this war as well as in the
previous one he had directed attention to British military
penmen.[11]

If American officers in the Revolution failed to make
unique contributions to the art of war that would later be
elevated to the level of universal principles, if they chose to
borrow heavily from European studies, they nevertheless
were not slavish imitators in the manner of some nineteenth-
century American military men who fell under the spell of
Baron Jomini and various Prussian thinkers. Instead, Continental officers combined European practice with their own
firsthand encounters in arms and with the values of their own
society. In doing so, they introduced a pragmatic element to
the American military tradition, which would be ignored by
the McClellans and Hallecks but embraced by the Taylors,
Grants, Eisenhowers, Marshalls, and Bradleys.

Nathanael Greene unknowingly anticipated pragmatic
post-Revolutionary trends when he advised Washington
that "experience is the best of schools and the safest guide
in Human affairs, yet I am no advocate for blindly following
all the maxims of European policy; but where reason corre-
sponds with what custom has long sanctified, we may safely
copy their Example." Greene's words contain the genius of
Steuben, who recognized that Americans already had their

"Prejudices" about fighting; it therefore became necessary "to deviate from the principles adopted in the Euorpean Armies." As a result, he combined Prussian, British, and American experiences in teaching the Continentals everything from the manual of arms to marching in columns. Above all, Steuben found that American soldiers, regardless of background, expected better treatment than they considered the lot of European rank and file. Steuben's *Regulations*, commonly known as the "Blue Book," stipulated that a company commander's "first object should be, to gain the love of his men, by treating them with every possible kindness and humanity, enquiring into their complaints, and when well founded, seeing them redressed. He should know every man of his company by name and character."[12]

Thanks to Washington's faith in Steuben, the Prussian's new and improved procedures came at exactly the right time, after the main army had become somewhat demoralized by reversals at Brandywine and Germantown in 1777 and after it had become apparent that the sizable army planned in 1776 was never to be. In fact, failure to achieve the anticipated manpower goals and continuous fluctuation in troop strength necessitated the periodic combining and reordering of units, as in Massachusetts where thirty-seven different regiments existed at one time or another. Without the improvements brought by Steuben's reforms and the considerable degree of continuity in the officer corps later in the war, these developments would have greatly weakened the army.

A final point about the Washington-Steuben relationship concerns the latter's role as inspector general, which the American and the Prussian together shaped into a position where Steuben operated as Washington's "defacto chief of staff." They combined the duties of drillmaster with those previously performed by the mustermaster general, and the adjutant general. Robert K. Wright, who quite correctly

points to the gradual "Europeanization" of the Continental
army, nevertheless states that "the rise of the inspector general again demonstrates the flexibility exercised in the use
of European precedents." Washington and his lieutenants
"borrowed where appropriate, but they were not afraid to
be innovative."[13]

Whatever the mixture of influences on the Continentals,
the officers of the 5,500-man French force that united with
Washington for the siege of Yorktown in 1781 found their
American allies impressive in performance. The Marquis
de Chastellux, the second in command, poet, and philo-
sophe, stated that the American artillery "formed in parade,
in the foreign manner . . . each gunner . . . ready to fire."
The Pennsylvania Line looked "very martial . . . Each brigade had a band of music." The Comte de Clermont-Crè-
vecoeur discovered that American infantrymen were "quite
good. They stand fast under fire and give a good account of
themselves." To Jean-Baptiste Antoine de Verger, "the
American Continental troops" were "very war-wise and
quite well disciplined. . . . They have supreme confidence
in General Washington." But it was Chastellux, a general
himself, who displayed the keenest interest in observing and
assessing the American commander, whom he reported had
created an open, relaxed atmosphere among his staff. He
further noted that the officers at headquarters "unite much
politeness to a great deal of ability."[14]

If Washington maintained the confidence of the vast majority of the army, he also retained the respect of Congress,
but it was not invariably easy to hold the good will of both.
The reason was that civil-military relations were far from
tranquil and harmonious; in fact, they were probably more
strained at certain periods during the Revolution than at
any other time in our history, although some authorities
might wish to marshal a case for equally serious—if somewhat different—altercations during Reconstruction and the

Vietnam War. In the Revolution, civil-military problems involved both the relations between the army and Congress and the relations between the military and civilians elsewhere, including state and local authorities and the public at large. The subject is obviously too extensive for an in-depth analysis here; we will focus our treatment on matters in which Washington played a major role and was actually caught in the middle between the army and Congress. Yet we must also ask why civil-military relations were so strained and why, given their seriousness, no coup was attempted.

From the army's standpoint, there are some similarities between the military's complaints in the Revolution and the army's sources of dissatisfaction since then. Revolutionary generals' cries about inadequate weaponry and manpower would echo down through the next two centuries. It is doubtful whether a military bureaucrat or field commander has ever conceded that he was adequately provided with everything. Such negative contentions have always given the general a great alibi if campaigns went poorly or if the war was lost. From the view of some generals, at least, it was better to ask for twice as much as their true needs demanded in order to be guaranteed receipt of their actual requirements.[15] Even so, rarely were an army's material deficiencies so painfully evident as at Morristown and Valley Forge. That in itself sets the Revolution apart from other American conflicts.

So do other factors, elements of discord in future wars which were mainly absent in 1776. There were no significant disagreements over allocating resources for the respective armed services, since the miniscule Continental navy had no prospect of challenging openly the Queen of the Seas. Nor do we encounter serious altercations over military strategy separating soldiers and civilians, for the Americans were preoccupied with defensive responses to British invasions from Rhode Island to Georgia. (On occasion, however, congressmen individually or collectively interjected opinions on military decisions, such as when or where to fight, or condemned a general for his behavior—for example, General Arthur St. Clair's failure to hold Fort Ticonderoga and General Benjamin Lincoln's surrender of Charleston.) Then, too, in that technologically primitive age there were no debates over weapons systems. "Weapons"—period—was the cry!

Civil-military disputes had a much more personal quality during the Revolution than in later periods—personal because officers as a whole felt that individually and as a corps they had been grievously wronged and that most of their problems lay with Congress. Besides charges of favoritism to foreign officers, which became less of an issue after the second or third year, they complained of low pay, salaries in arrears, meager living allowances, and absence of a fixed plan of postwar compensation for their years of sacrifice in the common cause. Some of the officers would have rejoiced if Congress, regardless of public attitudes, had stretched its authority and ordered on a massive scale the seizing of necessary goods and supplies and if it had somehow overridden state laws to conscript men in sufficient numbers to give flesh to skeletal regiments. Some officers expressed deep bitterness toward large segments of the civilian sector; they believed that by their daily sacrifices and physical dangers they themselves were living up to the principles of the Revolution, whereas the home front busied itself with hoarding, profiteering, luxurious living, and avoidance of military service. Perhaps only the Vietnam War showed anything approaching analogous feelings of American officers toward the domestic scene, although surely Union and Confederate military men were aware of much apathy, disaffection, and war-weariness behind their own lines. It is fair to speculate that only in World Wars I and II was there a sign of almost universal enthusiasm from the public in behalf of an American war effort.

Some historians think that tensions between the Continental army and society soared to a nearly explosive level, threatening to consume the Revolution and all it stood for. "There is a terrible falling off in public virtue since the commencement of the present contest," complained Nathanael Greene in 1779. "The loss of Morals and the want of public spirit leaves" the army "almost like a Rope of Sand." Congress often became the scapegoat for all that went wrong. A condemnation of that legislative tribunal by General Charles Lee, third-ranking officer in the army at the time of the New York campaign of 1776, is revealing. "Congress," he fumed, "having no military men in their body are continully confounding themselves and everybody else in military matters." Lee's castigation of civilian leaders sounded like Washington's blasts at the governor and assembly of Virginia nearly two decades beforehand. For that matter, there has never been any letting up on the part of some military elements; every American war has witnessed attacks on politicians who do not quite understand how conflicts should be fought. Vietnam was definitely no exception.[16]

Save for the postwar compensation issue, nothing better illustrates the sensitivity of the military than the Conway Cabal, an alleged Congressional scheme in the winter of 1777–1778 to remove Washington as commander in chief in favor of General Horatio Gates, whose victory over Burgoyne at Saratoga was contrasted with Washington's reversals in Pennsylvania. Though some dissatisfied persons favored Gates's elevation, no organized movement against Washington occurred. But the Virginian and his loyal lieutenants, spending a miserable winter at Valley Forge and sensitive over recent defeats, saw devils where none existed.

Had Congress removed Washington, it is likely that the army would have suffered a psychological blow from which it would have never recovered, and his departure would have ignited a mass of resignations that might well have left the service almost totally bereft of leadership. No doubt it would have stimulated intrigue for command, since all groups within the army would never have agreed on a proper choice to succeed him. We simply have nothing that would have been comparable in our military history. Lincoln knew that McClellan was popular with the Army of the Potomac, and Truman anticipated the wrath that descended upon him for his removal of MacArthur. But in neither case did the outcome of a war hang in the balance because of the firing of a general. In any event, the cabal episode was distressing all around, because it exacerbated civil-military sensitivities and embarrassed both Washington and Congress.[17]

From all the military's criticism of Congress, what are we to conclude about the lawmakers' behavior? They obviously wished to win the war, not dangle on the gallows at Tyburn or keep company with Sir Walter Raleigh's ghost in the Tower of London. Recent scholarship has questioned, if not rejected outright, the once-fashionable notion that Congress based its major wartime decisions on ideological considerations, although the solons' concerns about corruption and strict accountability for public expenditures offer insights into the continuing influence of protestant cultural values and British radical whig ideas on the American political mind. Nor does it seem that party activity was so serious as previously contended. Just as English repression drove people of different views to work together during the opening rounds of the conflict, so too did the constraints of war inhibit the formation of tightly knit factions at later stages. Congress's errors were more the result of ignorance and inexperience than of any fear that an American Caesar might emerge from the conflict.[18] Some of its most costly mistakes were made while endeavoring to improve the supply services by shifting major responsibility between the army departments and the states. That body would have bettered its record of war management had it not waited until a time of crisis but instead engaged in systematic, long-range planning.

The record of the states was worse. They often competed with the army quartermaster and commissary officers for goods, which they sometimes retained for their militias or used for the sole benefit of their own troops in the Continental line. For that matter, the states acted as though they were more ideologically motivated than Congress. Declares E. Wayne Carp: "state authorities' commitment to the welfare of their constituents, to the sanctity of private property, to the liberties of the inhabitants, and to the primacy of the civil power over the military was so strong that at times it appears they would rather have lost the war than compromised their principles." (All these home-front frustrations would reappear between 1861 and 1865 for Jefferson Davis and the military leaders of the Confederacy.)[19]

Such parochial state attitudes not infrequently led to clashes with Congress, which was an extralegal assembly only functioning with the sufferance of these same political entities. Not only was there an inadequate governmental structure to meet the military's material needs, but there was also no adequate way to present the military's views— no vehicle for meaningful communication, for an exchange of opinions on subjects that legitimately concerned the armed forces. (Poor communication existed even though Congress hustled several committees to Washington's camp and groups of officers sometimes dispatched petitions enumerating their complaints to the lawmakers.)

Under our federal Constitution of 1787, these matters are the ultimate responsibility of the president of the United States. They are partly delegated, as the chief executive sees fit, to the departmental secretaries and the chiefs of staff of the different services. What might be designated as administrative channels or the "pipeline" were missing in the Revolution. Frustrated generals were thus likely to sound off either publicly or privately in letters to congressmen, the contents of which invariably leaked if the recipient himself did not deliberately air them. Delegate Stephen Hopkins of Rhode Island, fed up with self-serving missives from officers, allegedly complained that "he never knew a General Quillman good for anything."[20] Several commanders such as Arnold and Charles Lee seemed to cultivate a genius for irritating civilians in and out of public life, and they exploited it to the hilt. Their outbursts pained Washington and did the army's cause more harm than good. Its fortunes also suffered when a military man endeavored to snuggle up to members of Congress in hopes of securing patrons, as did Horatio Gates.

Of course, had Washington behaved in a heavy-handed fashion out of frustration, his relations with both Congress and the states would have deteriorated. Unquestionably, he had it in his power to confirm the suspicions that doctrinaire whigs harbored toward all military men, at the same time that he would have betrayed the trust that Congress had placed in him during the first year of the war. In short, the conduct of Washington himself was a partial explanation for the fact that Congress was more pragmatic than ideological, that the underlying radical whig mindset of many of its members did not block cooperation between Washington and that body, although the legislators at times moved too slowly in Washington's view, glacially in the army's view.

Washington was literally the man in the middle, between an army with a multitude of complaints and grievances that ebbed and flowed in their intensity and a Congress that considered all too many officers impatient, unmindful of how deliberative bodies work, and generally insensitive to

Congress's weak muscle and meager resources. As a result, the lawmakers believed it desirable to keep some distance between the army and civil authority, in order to remind the military of the separate, superior station of civil government and to keep the army from trying to ingratiate itself with the politicians to win favor and influence.

Appointed by and responsible to Congress and a former member of that body, Washington was also the commander in chief of the army, which must not be allowed either to fall apart or to challenge civil control and which was entitled to have its just concerns articulated before Congress. Never again would an American military commander have such enormous burdens both unique and critical in nature. As best he could, he faced the task of compensating for the lack of those administrative channels that at a later time would serve as a filter for the resolution of civil-military misunderstandings and controversies. He had to explain the army to Congress and explain Congress to the army along with his other manifold duties, which in themselves seemed overwhelming. General Horatio Gates lamented during the Saratoga campaign that "a general of an American Army must be everything; and that is being more than one man can long sustain."[21]

Washington's responsibilities might be summarized thus: to sustain an army; to drum up new recruits every spring while enticing the much-abused militia to hold the lines in the interim months; to procure sufficient provisions, uniforms, tents, guns and ammunition. All these tasks entailed endless appeals to civilian leaders not only in Congress but at the state and local levels as well. A scavenger, Washington faced the additional challenge of wiring together his heterogeneous throng, making it fight and occasionally win—all without unduly antagonizing civilians and public officials. Yet he prevailed over these internal obstacles and the British foe alike. Any explanation for it must acknowledge valuable lessons learned during his career as a colonial soldier, his experiences during the siege of Boston, and his example and deeds as commander in chief throughout the war.

It is no wonder that his surviving correspondence is staggering in quantity, one of the reasons for Freeman's only slightly exaggerated assertion that the Virginian was nine-tenths administrator and one-tenth fighting general. His waking hours often were all but consumed with what now would be considered staff matters. Literally thousands of his letters from the war years have been preserved and fill nearly twenty-five volumes in the Fitzpatrick edition of his *Writings*. The published papers of no commanding general in American history—either those completed or those currently in progress—are so extensive as Washington's.[22]

Being faithful to his superiors and dedicated to the concept of civil supremacy did not mean that Washington failed to express his views on issues of great importance or dissent strongly when he disagreed with a congressional decision. Generals in free societies need not be "yes" men; nonetheless, if their thinking is rejected, they must carry out disagreeable orders and policies or else resign their commissions. Washington's occasional expression of such opinions through properly constituted routes was a positive contribution to our military heritage.

In a number of instances Washington spoke his mind and laid it on the line, so to speak. While he admitted that the army's seemingly endless dissatisfaction might well exasperate Congress, he reminded the members that they were engaged in no short, decisive contest, that the army spent most of its days in quarters struggling to exist on bare necessities. A "state of inactivity . . . will give leisure for cherishing their discontents and dwelling upon all the hardships of their situation." There was time—too much time—to listen to reports of profiteering or trading with the enemy on the home front. "The large Fortunes acquired by numbers out of the Army, affords a contrast that gives poignance to every inconvenience from remaining in it," he warned. Repeatedly, as early as January 1778 he urged Congress to devise a meaningful plan of postwar compensation for the army, and he minced no words on the correctness of that course or the animated feelings of the officers on that subject.[23]

Having gained more than "a small knowledge of human nature" during the French and Indian War, Washington reminded Congress that "interest" was much more a determinant of behavior than "public virtue." It was a truth unpalatable to idealistic Americans. They believed that the Revolution, based as it was on republican principles, could only be true to its goals if there existed a national character noted for its strong moral virture; they also thought that the Revolution would surely fail without such a character that meant—in terms of daily living and human relationships— honesty, bravery, devotion, and sacrifice. Washington was usually too circumspect to say in his public correspondence how naïve that kind of thinking was if pressed too far, how it could exceed the reality of the human condition. But in various letters to Congress he did point to the failure of thousands of the rank and file to reenlist and to the mass of officer resignations which seemed to reach floodlike proportions.

The Revolution undoubtedly needed idealism, but it also required common sense and practicality, both of which the Virginian possessed in full measure. He did not say that public virtue was a myth; he did indicate that it could carry the overwhelming part of mankind only so far, even in a republic. It could not exclusively govern conduct for interminable periods, particularly when people were confronted with wrenching sacrifices to themselves and their families. Washington commented directly on this problem: "I do not mean to exclude altogether the Idea of Patriotism. I know it exists, and I know it has done much in the present Contest. But I will venture to assert, that a great and lasting War can never be supported on this principle alone. It must be aided by a prospect of Interest or some reward. For a time, it may, of itself push Men to Action; to bear much, to encounter difficulties; but it will not endure unassisted by Interest."[24]

As for other matters, Washington informed the law-makers that too many foreign officers of doubtful qualifications had been given Continental commissions and placed above more deserving American officers, although he did so in language more restrained than the heated epistles to Congress on that score by Generals Greene, Sullivan, and Knox. While normally avoiding controversies between individual generals and their civilian masters, he came to Greene's defense when difficulties between the Rhode Islander and the legislators over the former's handling of the quartermaster department threatened to drive Greene from the army. In Washington's judgment, Greene was too valuable to lose. His subordinate's brilliant campaign in the South would justify the Virginian's intervention. Washington never denied that the problem of trying to keep the army supplied was a nightmare and that the failings of the system were not wholly the fault of either Congress or the supply officers. He did object vigorously, however, to the lawmakers' decision in 1779 to shift the responsibility for provisioning the army to the states, the results of which he accurately called "pernicious beyond description." When Congress sought to change the previously accepted terms for releasing the survivors of Burgoyne's army in America, Washington termed their actions unethical. Consequently, the legislators backed down, in part at least.[25]

So often did the commander in chief express such forthright opinions that he felt compelled to reiterate his intentions, as he stated to the president of Congress on April 3, 1780: "I hope I shall not be thought to have exceeded my duty in the unreserved manner in which I have exhibited our situation. Congress I flatter myself will have the goodness to believe that I have no other motives, than a zeal for the Public service, a desire to give them every necessary information, and an apprehension for the consequences of the evils we now experience."[26]

Because Congress recognized his loyalty and lack of personal ambition, he could more effectively voice his criticisms and concerns. But how best could he get them across? Normally he addressed his sentiments to the president of Congress, but that official was not necessarily the most prestigious or influential member of the tribunal; after the resignation of John Hancock in 1777, the post usually changed hands at least annually. Washington thus had to form a new working relationship with each congressional president: Henry Laurens of South Carolina, John Jay of New York, Samuel Huntington of Connecticut, Thomas McKean of Delaware, John Hanson of Maryland, Elias Boudinot of New Jersey, and Thomas Mifflin of Pennsylvania. It was hardly an accident that no two presidents came from the same state and that there was considerable variation in their abilities. As James Madison tartly observed in 1781, "the principle of rotation" seemed to be followed for no better reason than to enable as many states as possible to have an occupant of the presidential chair.[27]

Once again we see the institutional constraints upon communication between the central government (such as it was) and the army, whose responsible spokesman had to be Washington owing to the absence of later offices and agencies which would perform that function after 1789. Consequently, Washington resorted to yet another method, one which would be frowned on today and which caused serious problems for other generals in subsequent American history, most notably General MacArthur. Washington believed he had no alternative, and he was probably right. He began the practice, as early as July 1775, of occasionally writing letters to members of Congress and sometimes expressing views more bluntly than he thought appropriate in his missives to the president of that body. Certainly he did not behave like Congressman Hopkins's "General Quillman." Nor did he intrigue with factions as he had against Governor Dinwiddie in the 1750s. There are no references to "Chimney Corner Politicians," as was true of his epistles in the French and Indian War. While he showed no favoritism to his own state as commander in chief (in fact, Generals Daniel Morgan and George Weedon may have felt their careers suffered because they, like Washington, hailed from the Old Dominion), he seems to have felt more comfortable in passing on his views to Virginia congressmen, at first to Richard Henry Lee and later to Benjamin Harrison and Joseph Jones.[28]

Washington, as we saw in the previous chapter, had found in his initial dealings with New Englanders and in his labors to persuade Congress to establish an army for the duration, that tact and diplomacy were essential parts of his job. He walked a tightrope not only in his endeavors to explain the army and Congress to each other, but in other ways as well. Though carrying an all-embracing title, his duties and responsibilities were not precisely defined, particularly in relation to military commands outside the theater of his own operations. There have always been problems of jurisdictional boundaries in American wars. They have included the exact relationship between commanding generals or chiefs of staff and field commanders as Halleck and Grant would have confirmed in the Civil War, March and Pershing in World War I, and the joint chiefs of staff and MacArthur in the Korean War. But, unlike the Revolution, there was always a president as *the* commander in chief, assisted by a secretary of war or (after World War II) a secretary of defense, to help determine responsibilities and lines of authority.[29]

Washington, finding his own way, sometimes chose not to involve himself in the gray areas of decision-making, often because the issues were sensitive and controversial or because he lacked firsthand knowledge of a problem. He could assert, quite correctly, that almost all his service was in the region designated by Congress as the Middle Department (as opposed to the New England, Northern, Southern, and Western Departments). He usually declined to nominate commanders to head the various departments, so that he would avoid offending both the generals who were not chosen and their congressional friends. He declined to express his opinions about certain persons and events; he never recommended job-seeking civilians to Congress; and he never indicated, should anything happen to him, who his successor should be.

Congress on several occasions between 1776 and 1778 temporarily invested Washington with what contemporaries described as "dictatorial power." The lawmakers did so in crisis situations, after a British victory and/or after the virtual collapse of a state government, as in Pennsylvania following the twin American reversals at Brandywine and Germantown. These powers included at one time or another the authority to raise units and commission officers without state approval, to arrest people who refused to accept Continental currency, to confiscate provisions and equipment for his regiments without following state regulations, and to impose martial law on civilians.

For the most part, however, Washington was uncomfortable with such awesome authority, and he had no stomach for taking draconian steps, even in a revolution and war of survival. Only rarely did he turn to his new arsenal of home-front weapons, and wisely so. On the one occasion he acted like a proconsul—calling on all men who had recently taken an oath to George III now to swear allegiance to America or withdraw "themselves and families" to enemy lines—he was lambasted by Congressman Abraham Clark of New Jersey for overriding state jurisdiction. (Interestingly enough, Clark, a frequent military critic, could nevertheless temper his harsh words with a remark that makes us mindful of Gates's caveat on the burdens inherent in American generalship. Clark added that Washington was "too much incumbered to attend to every thing.")[30]

The impressment of goods owing to acute military shortages could never be entirely avoided, regardless of whether Washington was acting with temporary dictatorial powers. Yet, save for the Valley Forge winter, the Virginian managed to refrain from that practice on a large scale before 1779. Even when impressing, the supply officers under Washington's immediate control made every effort to obey state laws on the subject. Quartermaster and commissary agents petitioned local magistrates for permission before taking a farmer's wagon or grains, for which the man was given a certificate and ultimately compensated. To Washington, there were several reasons for holding the seizure of property to the barest minimum. First, confiscation might create in his own army "a disposition to licentiousness, plunder, and Robbery." Second, it "excited the greatest alarm and uneasiness, even among our best and warmest friends," to say nothing of spreading "disaffection, jealousy and fear in the people." Finally, confiscation contradicted revolutionary principles, a revolution which had its first visible beginnings in colonial opposition to British taxation programs of the 1760s. Citing John Locke, the great interpreter of the Glorious Revolution of 1688, Americans had asserted that men's property could not be taken from them without their consent, offered either as individuals or by their representatives. As Washington recalled for the benefit of his soldiers, it was "for the preservation of [their] own Rights," which included "Property," that the war was being fought.[31]

The year 1780—which may have been the Revolution's nadir, with Congress relying on the states for supplying the army, with inflation soaring to record levels, with the fall of Charleston and Arnold's treason—saw efforts to give Washington new and more sweeping powers than ever before. Significantly, these initiatives did not come from the army, which was assuredly suffering more than any other element in the country. In 1780 the army, in fact, sought "civilian solutions to military problems," as Carp nicely phrases it, petitioning Congress to provide the leadership to put the Revolution back on track.[32] Rather, the momentum began with individuals and political bodies at the state level. The New York assembly urged Congress to instruct Washington to move against "any State . . . deficient in furnishing" its "Quota of Men, Money, Provisions, or other Supplies." New York was unambiguous about his methods; he should by military force "compel it to furnish its deficiency." Similar language emanated from New York and New England representatives meeting at Hartford in November of 1780. It has been suggested that these measures were designed in substance to make Washington a "military dictator" and that Congress would have complied had he wanted such vast autonomy.[33]

There was unquestionably some support for the plan of the Hartford convention in Congress, although there were likely divergent opinions about how to implement it. In March 1781, a committee composed of James Madison, James Duane, and James Varnum proposed an amendment to the Articles of Confederation "to compel" delinquent "States to fulfill their federal engagements." Some members felt that the Articles, broadly interpreted, already allowed coercion of wayward states. Richard Henry Lee, a former congressman who once had been close to Washington and was alleged to have joined the pro-Gates group in 1777, implored the Virginia delegation at Philadelphia to follow the lawmakers' precedent of 1776–1778 and bestow upon Washington the muscle to make the states behave responsively.[34]

Of course, we cannot be sure what would have happened if Washington had asked for a grant of extraordinary authority, but he did not, and there is not the slightest evidence that he gave any encouragement to such maneuverings in 1780 and 1781. In his customary manner, he sought to strengthen the hand of Congress without expanding his own jurisdiction or arousing civilian sensitivities concerning the military's role.[35]

As the War of Independence drew to a close, both in Congress and in the army voices of compromise and moderation prevailed in the hammering out of national policies. Congress showed its concern for the welfare of the army, partly through the leadership of several former Continental generals who now sat in that body, partly through the leadership of Robert Morris, whom Congress had wisely chosen as superintendent of finance. In February 1783 Washington declared, "I . . . have the satisfaction of seeing the Troops better covered, better clothed, and better fed, than they have ever been in any former Winter Quarters."[36] Yet it was at this very time when its material wants were being addressed that there occurred the most serious mischief undertaken by a part of the army: a scheme to employ the military to bolster Congress—to do so not necessarily at the expense of civil supremacy but rather at the expense of the states. Certain nationalists in and out of Congress, including public creditors and junior army officers, found common ground or (one should say) a common enemy: the thirteen state governments. The alliance, such as it was, sought to pressure Congress and the states to strengthen the federal hand, which in turn would have enabled the lawmakers to deal with such unresolved issues as army backpay and a final determination of the half-pay arrangement agreed to earlier but now threatened by a lack of Continental revenues. Congressman James Madison heard reports that Washington had "become extremely unpopular among almost all [army] ranks from his known dislike of any unlawful proceeding" and that "many leading characters" were working to have Gates replace him.[37] Whether the gossip-spreaders believed their own tales or merely wished to frighten state and federal politicians is unclear.

If subsequent events were to show that Washington was never in firmer control, he nonetheless read the apprehensive mood of the army as it faced the prospect of being disbanded before its crucial concerns were satisfactorily resolved. "The temper of the Army," he confided to Joseph Jones, "has become more irritable than at any period since the commencement of the War. This consideration alone, prevented me . . . from requesting leave to spend this Winter in Virginia, that I might give some attention to my long neglected private concerns."[38]

The movement now known as the Newburgh Conspiracy (the army was in winter cantonment at Newburgh on the Hudson) failed for a number of reasons, including the unwillingness of almost all the general officers to participate. Henry Knox's response might well have become something of a creed for the American army, as valid for our day as for his: "I consider the reputation of the American Army as one of the most immaculate things on earth," he declared; "we should even suffer wrongs and injuries to the utmost verge of toleration rather than sully it in the least degree."[39]

In retrospect, we can say there was no plan for a military coup, not even a well-organized group within the army to push its claims; nor is it clear that the army would have refused to disband before its concerns were dealt with, which may well have been the greatest apprehension of those who were fearful of the military in early 1783.[40]

Even so, had Washington ignored the discontent or given tacit sympathy to the inflammatory Newburgh Addresses, which used menacing language to call for greater unity of the army in pressing its case with Congress, he could have greatly exacerbated the situation. Given such a scenario, one can scarcely imagine what might have been the possible course of events. At the very least, had the essence of the harsh Addresses been adopted by the officer corps, forwarded by Washington, and resulted in quick, affirmative action by Congress, the outcome would have set a dangerous precedent for the intervention of the American military in the political and constitutional processes of the nation. Washington wasted no time in appearing before the assembled officers and persuading them to allow him to help place their legitimate grievances before the Continental Congress in a respectful manner—an episode that may well have been the most dramatic scene of the war. (It was a war, one should add, that had more than its share of memorable happenings, including Washington's moving farewell to his officers at Fraunces Tavern in New York City when the army disbanded.) At Newburgh, a tense moment in the Revolution turned into a very emotional one when Washington, well into his firm but conciliatory remarks, hesitated, pulled out his new spectacles, and put them on. Many did not realize that his sight had become impaired. As he fumbled in adjusting his glasses, he intoned apologetically, "Gentlemen, you will permit me to put on my spectacles, for I have not only grown gray but almost blind in the service of my country."[41]

His performance further illustrates two points made earlier: his fine sense of the dramatic and his role as intermediary between Congress and the army. In both respects, it was his finest hour. Indeed, a reading of his general orders and letters to the lawmakers over the period March 12 to March 30 reveals how effective he was. To the officers, he stressed his conviction that the delegates in Philadelphia entertained the most "exalted sentiments" about the army. "But, like all other large Bodies, where there is a variety of different Interests to reconcile, their deliberations are slow." To the Congress, he emphasized the officers' respectful approach and fair-minded proposals (adopted March 15, the day he appeared before them), which he forwarded with a vigorous supporting letter. During those seemingly critical days he also resorted to his occasional tactic of communicating directly with influential members of the federal tribunal. When Congress, on March 22, commuted the half-pay for life bonuses into full salaries for five years in the form of interest-bearing government securities, he immediately reproduced that legislative resolution in full in his general orders.[42] It had not been the only matter in dispute between Congress and the army, but it was the most sensitive one at that time; its settlement paved the way for dealing with other difficulties before the army was disbanded. Commutation, a most reasonable solution, showed the moderation of the army, since the officers themselves had proposed essentially the same idea even before the Newburgh Addresses. In so doing they had displayed sensitivity for civilian apprehensions about the earlier scheme of half-pay for life. More than a few Americans, not just doctrinaire anti-army elements, saw this scheme as either beyond the authority of Congress or unhealthy in a republic since it would create a distinct class of pensioners.[43]

Washington actually sliced to the core of the Newburgh Conspiracy. He believed that a cluster of politicians allied to public creditors sought to manipulate the army on their own ends. Although he doubted that the dissidents, civilian or military, were out to impose rule by the sword, an army was nonetheless "a dangerous instrument to play with," as he bluntly warned Congressman Alexander Hamilton.[44] Washington's attack on manipulative politicians and businessmen has on occasion been repeated in our subsequent history—when, for example, critics have accused national administrations and their followers of seeking a bloated military establishment to stimulate the economy or to pursue an adventurous foreign policy or have accused them of creating a military-industrial complex.

At Newburgh, and throughout much of the war, Washington had to contend with officers highly critical of the behavior of civilian governments and the attitudes and values of society in general, notions which for some of his subordinates bordered on isolation, if not alienation, from their fellow countrymen. It was they who had saved the Revolution! If no more than a handful of his military comrades were ready to redress their grievances by armed force, many others—according to Charles Royster—saw themselves as more entitled than other parts of society to define the goals of the nation and offer wisdom on such matters as federal-state relations and constitutional reform. Since this is hardly an unusual human feeling, to believe that one's own experiences may offer meaningful insights into broader realms, his judgment may be overly harsh but not without an element of truth. As Royster says, "The wartime experience of the military underlay the first formulation of the claim that a few patriots could wield special authority as saviors of the republic. The Continental officers' patriotic professionalism may exemplify the recurring pattern in American history in which a group or faction of patriots claimed to be the sole embodiment of the ideals of the American Revolution [and the nation.]"[45]

If there is a lesson here, it is that rarely does one body or organization by virtue of its experience, its morality, or its suffering and sacrifice gain the right to speak for us all. Nor should greater weight automatically be given to its opinions—be it the American Civil Liberties Union, the Americans for Democratic Action, the National Council of Churches, the Moral Majority, or the Pentagon. Each has and should vigorously exercise the right to articulate its thinking in the marketplace of free ideas, from which national decisions must ultimately be shaped. With this idea General George C. Marshall, another enlightened soldier, would surely have agreed. Since "national defense" was such "a tremendously expensive business," he declared on the eve of World War II, "I think it is the business of every mature citizen to acquaint himself with the principal facts, and form a general idea as to what he or she thinks is the wise course for this country to follow."[46] The ability of both Washington and Marshall to put defense and war-making considerations into broad perspective suggests that the American military has never been a monolith; that the military, like other interest groups and institutions, has had its myopic and farsighted elements.

This truism has not always been easy for Americans to acknowledge, particularly in the eighteenth century—not only because of their anti-army intellectual baggage, with both its classical and British roots, but also because a national form of constitutional democracy was not yet a point of reference for all Americans as it had become long before the Civil War. Even in the 1860s, however, one encounters serious apprehensions that democracy might fall victim to what Walt Whitman called that strange, sad war. More recent conflicts have generated concerns about the preservation of civil liberties and the unwarranted influence of the armed forces, although there have scarcely been predictions of possible military takeovers except in an occasional novel such as *Seven Days in May.*

Tensions mount and multiply in a protracted conflict like

the Revolutionary War, which was unmatched in its longevity before Vietnam. Congress continued to be an extralegal forum until the ratification of the Articles of Confederation in 1781. The thirteen states, prior to and after ratification, hardly set Washington and the army an example for fidelity to the federal legislature, since they responded so slowly and sometimes not at all to its appeals for men and supplies. Only a stable, firmly institutionalized civilian regime can easily avoid military pressure and rule. In what sense, then, would the Continental army have acted illegally or unconstitutionally if in one form or another it had threatened Congress or endeavored to change the political system? After all, a revolution was in progress, and the twists and turns of violent upheavals are not easy to chart or predict. If history teaches anything since 1776, it is surely that.

If all had turned out well, some Americans were nonetheless troubled by the realization that the prescription for victory was so at variance with radical whig theory. The militia had not carried the sizable burden for defense assigned to it in Anglo-American mythology. The same patriots were concerned that men did not join the Continental service in massive numbers, which would have meant—in their view—no need to recruit a long-term army. That army, as it turned out, eventually had to enlist much of its rank and file from the lower orders of society, surely a troubling departure from the radical whig notion that upstanding, independently minded farmers and artisans should form the backbone of the army. A number of these idealistic citizens—precisely how many is unclear—went so far as to deny the army the very handsome share of the victory that was rightfully its own in 1783. They did so because they believed it unhealthy, possibly even dangerous, to praise an army that seemed too professional. Royster, who has examined this strain of revolutionary thought, phrases it well: "Americans reclaimed the war from the army to whom they had tried to entrust it, and they showed how the people had won the

war together. The future security of American independence would rest not on a military establishment but on
public virtue. To believe that public virtue had the strength
to sustain independence, Americans wanted to believe that
public virtue had won it."[47]

But such attitudes appear to have been more prevalent
with state-level officials and other pen-wielding civilians
than with Congress itself. The evidence indicates that the
greatest volume of anti-army rhetoric came from states that
were most heavily affected by the presence of Washington's
army and consequently felt most severely its requirements
for aid and succor. Congressmen from those states also
sometimes joined the clamor against undue military influence in the domestic sector. In criticizing Washington—or
more commonly his subordinates, especially in the supply
departments—they often resorted to language that was not
always fair or appropriate in an American context. It was
language laced with radical whig references to standing armies robbing citizens of their freedoms, or serving as instru-
ments of corruption, or turning citizen-recruits into myr-
midons blindly following the commands of their officers and
becoming permanently alienated from their own society.
Such references were no more accurate than some of the
simplistic criticisms that the military directed at the civilian
sector.

In reading the correspondence of the period, particularly
private letters, one almost has the feeling that every revolutionary appeared to be sniping at every other revolutionary,
to have been forgetful that it was the British and not fellow
Americans who wore the red coats. The American Revolution has been called liberal, moderate, and conservative in
character. Why not describe it as a cantankerous revolution
as well, though we will need to concede that it showed fewer
internal fractures than most revolutionary wars elsewhere
in the last two centuries?

Washington, ever the man in the middle, better understood the kind of military tensions that are inherent in free and open societies than did most of his countrymen, soldiers or civilians. He, above all others, labored successfully to keep those tensions from getting out of hand. And he did so, as the Comte de Rochambeau marveled, despite "an untenable military constitution." Though it was seldom acknowledged then, he proved that a professional army was not incompatible with civil liberty. In 1697 the English radical whig John Trenchard had written of the danger with standing armies: "The Constitution must either break the Army, or the Army will destroy the Constitution." Trenchard's fear did not come home to rest in the American Revolution. Congressman James Varnum was rightly skeptical when he doubted that "political and civil liberty can be enjoyed amidst the Din of arms, in their utmost platonic Extent." But Americans in the Revolution came far closer to preserving civil liberty than one would have expected in an upheaval of that nature; much of the credit was owing to Washington and his army. It was a Washington-shaped army, and when it complained, it wanted pay not power. To some of his troubled countrymen, it looked too much like a European army, but it had not sought traditional Old World objectives of empire and glory.[48]

Outside the Anglo-American framework the idea of civil control of the military had little if any meaning. From the time that it took its modern form in late seventeenth-century England, the concept had never been severely tested by the pressures of a divisive war that strained Britain to the breaking point. It was in America rather than in the mother country that such a test first took place, between 1775 and 1783. The Revolution also marked the development of a corollary to the doctrine of civil control: namely, that warfare had to be conducted in a manner reasonably consistent with the ideals of the country and the rights of its citizens.

What Massachusetts authorities had said in praise of

Washington in 1776—that he had respected the "constitution of this colony"—now might be expressed in behalf of the nation. That is what President Thomas Mifflin meant when Washington resigned his commission to Congress, then meeting at the Maryland State House in Annapolis. "You have," said Mifflin, "conducted the great military contest with wisdom and fortitude invariably regarding the civil power and through all disasters and changes."[49] Given the mindset of Americans then, could Congress have given its retiring Cincinnatus a greater compliment?

FOUR

George Washington and George Marshall

ONE FINDS THE LEGACY OF GEORGE WASHINGTON TO THE American military tradition best exemplified by General George C. Marshall. Both are commonly thought of as Virginians, and Marshall has been referred to as the last of the Virginians. If, in truth, Marshall was a Pennsylvanian by birth—he admitted that his nasal twang gave him away—there was much of Virginia in his life. His home, Uniontown in western Pennsylvania, was once part of Virginia's vast claim to the Ohio Valley. Because of that claim, Washington had fought in the immediate region of Marshall's youth. As a schoolboy Marshall had hunted and fished at locations where Washington had vanquished a small French party under Sieur Coulon de Jumonville, where Washington later built Fort Necessity and had then himself capitulated to the Gallic enemy, and where Washington and others had buried Braddock following his defeat. A distant relative of Chief Justice John Marshall, George Marshall had family roots in Virginia. He graduated from Virginia Military Institute; moreover, having expressed a desire like Washington's to enjoy a simple, bucolic life after a long career of public service, he retired in 1945 to a Virginia country seat. Dodona Manor at Leesburg, an imposing old dwelling that had once belonged to Washington's grandnephew, was to be his own Mount Vernon. There he would rest and reflect, to quote Washington metaphorically, under "my own vine and fig tree" (or with his beloved roses and tomato plants as Marshall would have expressed it). Both genuinely wished to escape the limelight; having no desire to profit further from their past accomplishments, they rejected appeals from publishers and well-wishers to pen their memoirs. In Marshall's case, the offer of one million dollars from the *Saturday Evening Post* came when he had thirteen hundred dollars in the bank.[1]

Neither general, however, was destined to see his dream of solitude and privacy gratified at war's end. Ever selfless and responsible, they could not decline when duty again beckoned in a different form. Washington became the nation's first president, and Marshall headed a postwar mission to China before serving as secretary of state and secretary of defense in the Truman administration. Something about their personal character explained their willingness to come forth once more in behalf of their country, and it is in the realm of character that the Virginia connection between Washington and Marshall rests most firmly in the public mind. Marshall, like Washington and the other great Virginians of his generation and like Robert E. Lee as well, was thought to be a rock of stability, completely dedicated and committed to the cause he espoused.

The fact that the native and the adopted Virginian were remote and aloof rather than gregarious added to the aura that surrounded each man. The fact that both were named George is hardly noteworthy, for both as adults discouraged first-name familiarity and could be downright chilling to those who tried to breach their inner walls. Perhaps the point about eschewing familiarity is best made with anecdotes.

While participating in the Constitutional Convention at Philadelphia in 1787, several delegates were commenting on Washington's reserved, distant manner. The bold and witty Gouverneur Morris felt that his colleagues had exaggerated and remarked that he was as intimate with Washington as with his closest friends. Alexander Hamilton then issued Morris a challenge, offering to provide wine and supper at his own expense if Morris would approach Washington, slap him on the back, and say, "My dear General, how happy I am to see you look so well." On the designated occasion, Morris carried out his part of the bargain, although evidently with a degree of diffidence that had scarcely been expected in view of his earlier expression of confidence. Morris stepped up to Washington, bowed, shook hands, and gingerly placed his left hand on Washington's shoulder. "My dear General," said Morris, "I am very happy to see you look so well." Washington's reaction was instantly frigid. Removing the hand, he stepped back and glared silently at the abashed Morris as the assemblage watched in embarrassment.[2]

The Washington anecdote, however revealing of the man's normal posture, may be apocryphal, but our Marshall story is authentic. At his first official conference with President Franklin D. Roosevelt in 1938, Marshall (the freshly minted deputy chief of staff) was asked a leading question about air power with which he did not agree. Roosevelt, thinking he had made an effective case for a priority in planes, said, "Don't you think so, George?" Marshall eyed the President icily and replied, "Mr. President, I am sorry, but I don't agree with that at all." Roosevelt, who first-named one and all, never again addressed Marshall as anything but general. Marshall himself recounted later, "I wasn't very enthusiastic over such a misrepresentation of our intimacy."[3]

Because Marshall is so close to us in time, and because of the splendid volumes of Forrest Pogue, we may have a more accurate appreciation of Marshall's contributions to our military heritage than of Washington's. It may come as no surprise to say that, with few exceptions, serious civilian historians have not displayed a consuming interest in Washington as a military man. What may be harder to explain is the lack of critical attention he has received from professional soldiers, who until fairly recently dominated the writing of military history in America; this is all the more unusual because military men have tended to be deeply conscious of history and its relevance. To study a famous battle is to simulate combat, to give officers a vivid sense of being present and engaging vicariously in a meaningful tactical exercise. It surely sharpens one's wits to be mindful of the need to anticipate unforeseen events or fortuitous circumstances. There is also the more important sense of involvement on a higher level in the examination of strategy that shaped campaigns and led to the battles. On becoming assistant commandant of the Infantry School at Fort Benning, Georgia, in 1927, Marshall made more rigorous an already existing requirement that every officer student prepare a short monograph on a military history subject. Marshall remembered that as a student himself at the Army Staff College he had devoted considerable attention to "past operations," particularly the Franco-Prussian War and the American Civil War; he made no mention, however, of assignments dealing with Washington's Revolutionary career.

Washington had become dated and irrelevant quite soon after the Revolution. Europeans, not Americans, continued to produce the influential military literature in the Western World, and there seemed to be nothing new and original in Washington's battles and campaigns. Broken down into its components, much of what had appeared novel about American warfare had antecedents in European light infantry, thin skirmish lines, and so on; moreover, no European monarchy thought it would have to engage in the type of struggle that confronted Britain in America in 1775. The War of Independence took place before the study of strategy was a recognized area of investigation. It became so with the emergence of Napoleon, who captured the imagination of scholar-soldiers everywhere; he was a practitioner of the offensive—the strategy of annihilation—rather than the defensive, as was usually the case with Washington. If Europeans ignored Washington the soldier, so did Americans, except for the popularizers and romantics. Serious military writers and thinkers on both sides of the Atlantic were under the hypnotic spell of a Swiss military intellectual, Baron Jomini, a founder of the strategic study of warfare who codified the lessons and principles of Napoleonic conflict. Even for Americans, writes Russell Weigley, "the object lessons were almost entirely Napoleonic and almost never Washingtonian. Early West Point strategists had their Napoleon Club, not their Washington Club. The first American books about strategy, Dennis Hart Mahan's and Henry W. Halleck's, contained much about Napoleon and little about Washington."[4]

Washington seemed to reveal other limitations for serious scholarly pursuits, and they too reflected the French impact on the United States army. Two increasingly important fields of military investigation, though predating Napoleon in origin, were artillery and engineering. In the post-1800 years military education was highly technical and scientific in nature—nowhere more so than at the new Military Academy. Both Jonathan Williams, the first superintendent, and Sylvanus Thayer, West Point's most influential superintendent, had observed the French military system by traveling to Europe; Thayer had returned to the banks of the Hudson with a thousand books for the cadet library. Washington, in contrast, had never received formal military schooling; prior to 1775 he had only held commissions in the Virginia forces, his combat activity confined to the frontier.

Serious-minded career officers also found Washington's personal example damaging to their ambitions for the army, since his own military background suggested to civil-

ians and militia advocates (oblivious to Napoleon and
Jomini) that extensive formal training in arms was unnecessary in a republic. Indeed, Washington's kind of soldier received Harvard's blessings—from President Charles W.
Eliot, who praised the Virginian's amateurish background,
and from Henry Cabot Lodge, class of 1871, who portrayed
Washington as a "fighting man" by nature, "hot blooded
and fierce in action," capable of learning what he needed to
master the martial arts on the battlefield itself.[5] In wartime
during the century after Washington's death the government continued to give high rank to amateurs with militia
backgrounds, men who in turn used their service records as
stepping-stones to the most elevated political offices. Seven
of these officers with predominantly domestic backgrounds
attained the presidency: Andrew Jackson, William Henry
Harrison, Franklin Pierce, Rutherford B. Hayes, James A.
Garfield, Benjamin Harrison, and William McKinley.

An officer corps that was not so professional as its most
professionally oriented members wished it to be—that is, as
professional as its French and German counterparts—was
not about to embrace Washington warmly. They faced
problems enough in an America that voiced the rhetoric of
democracy and equality, that looked ambivalently at best on
learned and specialized professions, be they law, medicine,
or arms.

America's rise to world power, from the Spanish-Ameri-
can War onward, brought no abrupt change in the historical
fortunes of the army's first commander in chief. When military writers did turn to Washington, they normally all but
ignored his French and Indian War years as well as other
factors that would serve to broaden his soldierly horizons,
such as his legislative responsibilities. So it was in books by
soldier-historians like Henry B. Carrington, Matthew Forney Steele, and William A. Ganoe. In his last revised edition
appearing in 1942, Ganoe lavished more attention on the

background and personal qualities of Douglas MacArthur
than he devoted to Washington. If the uniformed chroniclers
praised Washington (and, after a fashion, they all did), it was
most likely for his character: his "unswerving sense of duty,
his patience, tact, strength of purpose, patriotism, and tenacity"—as Steele phrased it.[6]

If few within the American military (even into the twentieth century) could admire Washington as a professional
soldier, they nevertheless saw a kind of negative relevance in
his inability to enlist great numbers of men for the duration of
the war, in his heavy reliance on poorly trained militia, and
in Congress's insistence on involving itself closely in aspects
of military decision-making, even though it lacked expertise
in managing a war effort. Here were valuable lessons for
their own day. Even in times of tranquillity the nation should
have a reasonably imposing military establishment, in order
to be better prepared in the event of conflict than Washington had been in the Revolution.

Of this self-serving literature Emory Upton's *The Military
Policy of the United States* stands in a class by itself, owing to
its profound influence on the officer mind of the Gilded Age
and well beyond. A West Point graduate, Upton compiled a
distinguished combat record in the Civil War. After a tour
as commandant of cadets at his alma mater, Upton went
abroad to examine Asian and European military establish-
ments and returned to write a devastating attack on American military attitudes and practices. The key to the country's mistaken approach lay in the Revolution, for the
American system—or lack of system—was rooted in the
War of Independence. Washington was Upton's star witness. Upton seemed to quote everything of a negative character that the Virginian had ever said about brief enlistments, irregulars, the states, and Congress—regardless of
their context, regardless of other conflicting remarks, regardless of the need to make allowance for frustrations of

the moment—in order to demonstrate that the Revolutionary military tradition was worthless. The military reform
crusader's list of fifteen "Lessons of the Revolution" constituted a litany of errors, most of which had been repeated
in succeeding American conflicts as well.[7]

Whereas Napoleon and Jomini were the heroes of Mahan
and Halleck, Upton and his followers favored the German
military model of Otto von Bismarck and Helmut von Moltke, whose armies had scored decisive victories over Austria
in 1866 and France in 1870 that culminated in the creation of
the modern German state. The military history of nation-
making in Germany appeared to offer much more that was
useful than the record of Washington and other American
revolutionists. Upton's proposed reforms, which he outlined
before a congressional committee, included a general staff
that would augment the authority of the army hierarchy at
the expense of the president and the secretary of war and a
substantially enlarged regular army. "It is difficult in reading Upton," observes Weigley, "not to believe that he would
have liked to confine the duties of civilian leaders in military
affairs to countersigning acts of the principal military commanders to assure their constitutionality."[8]

Ironically, Washington, whose own military background
and Revolutionary career seemed to offer little of a positive
nature, was quoted in defense of a somewhat Teutonic military structure that the American people refused to accept.
This is not to say, however, that most citizens were pacifists
or that many were ever really fearful of a military coup if the
armed forces were substantially expanded. They were preoccupied instead with keeping government small and taxes
low, and they assumed (quite accurately in the nineteenth
century at any rate) that after the War of 1812 America was
secure from European embroilments. The danger of a formidable armed establishment came less from the military
itself than from the politicians, who might be tempted to

employ a beefed-up army and navy in foreign adventures, including muscle-flexing in the Western Hemisphere. In retrospect, one may well conclude that peacetime defense spending, while never completely adequate, was fairly sensible before the great wars of the twentieth century. It was devoted to officer training at West Point and later service schools, to maintaining coastal fortifications and frontier posts, and to exploring the West.

There was, of course, nothing wrong with the fact that military intellectuals such as Mahan, Halleck, and Upton wrote as advocates of exacting professional standards and claimed that European doctrine had much to offer. It was imperative that the American officer corps possess the finest skills, since in national emergencies that corps would need to train and assimilate hosts of young men from civilian life into the armed forces. Had American military men been so disposed to follow an earlier German theorist, the Prussian Karl von Clausewitz, as they were to follow Jomini and Moltke, they might have given further concern to the uniquely American problems of defense and warfare. Revealing a breadth lacking in most military commentators, Clausewitz stressed throughout his magnum opus, *On War,* that armed conflict was merely an extension of politics. Instead, American military men ignored the record of Washington, who understood America's history and traditions, who consequently approached Congress tactfully during the Revolution about long-term recruits, and who in training his men was ever mindful of their civilian backgrounds.

Both civilian and military students of American wars have, to be sure, always praised Washington for his devotion to the concept of civil control of the military. Some Uptonians may have done so perfunctorily. But some soldiers were enthusiastic, as was General O. O. Howard in an 1881 article in the *United Service.* (Howard's article is a source of some interest, since military periodicals over the past one hundred and fifty years have all but excluded Washington from their pages.)[9] We can point out two most recent expressions on the subject, one by a civilian and one by a soldier. Above all else, writes Richard H. Kohn, "Washington should be remembered and appreciated for his absolute, unconditional, and steadfast refusal ever to seek or seize power outside legitimate political or constitutional channels." Indeed, "from the very beginning of his command, respect for civil authority was his first principle." General James L. Collins, Jr., states that "the example, the image, and even the legend of Washington have had an immense influence in shaping the American officer corps and in providing ideals of responsible leadership. I would point to General George C. Marshall, the World War II chief of staff, as a faithful follower of the Washington tradition."[10]

A civilian historian who saw a connection between Washington and Marshall was Douglas S. Freeman, the distinguished biographer of Robert E. Lee. Freeman, then at work on what would be his seven-volume life of Washington, hailed *Time*'s choice of Marshall as its "Man of the Year" for 1943. Freeman declared that Marshall's "noblest qualities" were virtually identical to those found in Jefferson's "famous characterization" of Washington. "As far as he saw," said Jefferson, "no judgment was ever sounder. . . . His integrity was most pure, his justice the most inflexible I have ever known, not motives of interest or consanguinity, of friendship or hatred being able to bias his decisions." "That is George Marshall," added Freeman, "that and much more besides." Harvard University also found a tie between Washington, who received an honorary doctorate of laws from that institution in 1776, and Marshall, who accepted the same degree in 1947 on the occasion of his so-called Marshall Plan commencement address outlining an American proposal for the postwar economic recovery of Europe. The latter's degree citation stated that in terms of character, integrity and respect for American ideals and institutions Marshall brooked comparison with only one other American: Washington.[11]

All the same, Washington-Marshall comparisons have not been numerous; even more surprising, those scholars conscious of defining an American military tradition have not paid particular heed to the two "Virginians." An essay by T. Harry Williams provides us with our point of departure for probing more deeply into comparative military analysis. In the aftermath of the Truman-MacArthur controversy of 1951, Williams argued that American military leaders have been either "Mac" or "Ike" types and that his preference was clearly for the latter. The "Ikes" were open and easygoing, friendly and sometimes folksy, attuned to the democratic ideals of the republic, and consequently comfortable and understanding in their relations with civilian superiors. Williams believed that Zachary Taylor, U. S. Grant, and Dwight D. Eisenhower represented the "Ike" heritage at its best. In contrast, the "Macs"—exemplified by Winfield Scott, George B. McClellan, and Douglas MacArthur—were haughty and cold, dramatic and even theatrical on occasion; their values and conduct derived from an older, elitist past. All of these qualities made it hard, if not impossible, for them to accept civilian control comfortably.[12]

Williams's essay provoked a critical response from Samuel P. Huntington in *The Soldier and the State*, an influential work on civil-military relations in America. Huntington considered Williams's thesis, while useful in some respects, "restricted in scope, failing to encompass important elements of the American military tradition which fall into neither the 'Ike' nor 'Mac' category." According to Huntington, the "Macs" and "Ikes" were actually two aspects of the tradition of political involvement on the part of the military. Declared Huntington, "the true opposition is not between the Taylor-Grant-Eisenhower line and the Scott-McClellan-MacArthur line, but rather between both of these, on the one hand, and the professional strand of American militarism (which might be described as the Sherman-Pershing-Ridgway line), on the other. Therefore, the real difference was between the 'Ike-Macs' and the 'Uncle Billies' or 'Black Jacks.' "[13]

Huntington's sympathies are with the professionals (as he defines them). The real hero of his book is Sherman, who served as commanding general of the army from 1869 to 1883. Huntington views Sherman as the father of modern military professionalism in America. Founder of what eventually became the Command and General Staff College at Fort Leavenworth and supporter of other military schools and service journals, Sherman considered Upton his protégé, and he supported before Congress his subordinate's ideas for military reform.

Perhaps we can unite the concepts of Williams and Huntington by saying that some generals fit into a political component of the American military tradition; the "Ikes" have behaved admirably in that respect and the "Macs" have, to say the least, been controversial. We can also maintain that other military leaders have made considerable efforts to eschew close ties to the civilian sector, because they felt (according to Huntington, in any case) that such involvement would compromise the integrity of the armed forces and detract from their endeavors to achieve a full measure of professionalism.

Did Williams and Huntington, though stimulating and provocative, tend to oversimplify the elements of the American military heritage? Is it, in fact, impossible for individual generals to represent the best of both aspects of the American military tradition? While not necessarily easy, it is possible, and the proof lies in the careers of Washington and Marshall.

For purposes of analysis, there are advantages to reversing the above-mentioned categories and discussing Hun-

tington's professionalism before turning to Williams's political component. Washington and Marshall benefited from
extremely important military experiences of a professional
nature before each became commander in chief at a most
critical period in American history: Washington in June
1775 soon after the beginning of the Revolutionary War,
which pitted the thirteen colonies against the most powerful
nation in the world; Marshall in September 1939, on the
very day that Hitler's juggernaut descended on Poland. Yet
some felt they had been cast in command roles beyond their
training and competence. Charles Lee, a veteran British officer and a former general of Catherine the Great, was regarded in some quarters as preferable to Washington.
Marshall, still a colonel as late as 1936, had been elevated
over the heads of senior brigadier and major generals in
1939. If Washington's only lengthy command had been at
the regimental level in the French and Indian War,
Marshall had not led a division in World War I.

An effort to treat Washington as a professional may raise
some eyebrows, since he never held a regular commission
prior to the Revolution and since military professionalism
as we think of it today dates from the generation of Jomini
and Clausewitz. Even so, these chapters have endeavored to
show that Washington behaved very professionally by the
standards of his time, both in the French and Indian War
and in the War of Independence. In the years between
those conflicts, he had not forgotten his appreciation of a
military life—he who had tried unsuccessfully to procure
for his home at Mount Vernon the busts of six great captains, including Alexander the Great, Julius Caesar, and
Frederick II of Prussia, and who had chosen in 1772 to be
attired in his old Virginia uniform for his first known portrait, doubtless the same uniform he wore at the opening
sessions of the Second Continental Congress as an indica-
tion of his willingness to fight for American liberties.

While we have stressed that Washington was a teacher in both wars, the teacher was not unwilling to learn from others, including Steuben. It is hardly insignificant that the officers who esteemed Washington most were themselves the most soldierly in their orientation: bright junior officers such as John Laurens and Alexander Hamilton, militarily self-educated senior officers such as Nathanael Greene and Henry Knox, conscientious European volunteers such as the Marquis de Lafayette and Steuben, and the officers of the French expeditionary army at Yorktown, particulary the Marquis de Chastellux.

Less effort is required to demonstrate Marshall's professional credentials. His résumé prior to World War II bulged with rich experiences, both at home and abroad: a tour in the Philippines; years as a student and teacher at the army schools of Fort Leavenworth; a second assignment in the Philippines; two years in Europe with the Allied Expeditionary Force during and after World War I; several years as special assistant to Chief of Staff John J. Pershing in the early 1920s; a stint in China; a period as instructor and administrator at the Infantry School at Fort Benning, as head of the Army War Plans Division, and as deputy chief of staff. His career spanned nearly forty years before he succeeded General Malin Craig as chief of staff in 1939.

In his service record and his attitude of mind Marshall was a professional soldier in the finest sense. He undoubtedly received his most valuable professional education (professional in Huntington's strictly military sense) during what was then known as the Great War. Though he had not emerged in 1918 with a star on his shoulder and a divisional command like MacArthur, he had participated from high ground. From the post of chief of operations and training for the First Division, he moved on to become chief of the operations division of the First Army. In the latter capacity, writes Forrest Pogue, "he had a key role in planning and

supervising the movement and commitment of more troops
in battle than any American officer would again achieve until General Omar Bradley established his 12th Army Group
in France in 1944."[14]

There are several noteworthy comparisons between
Washington and Marshall in terms of professionalism.
Strange though it may seem, Washington the young Virginia officer really thought of himself as a professional soldier and said as much. He was terribly frustrated by not
receiving regular status; for that reason as well as for other
difficulties, he seriously considered resigning from the Virginia service during the darkest days of the French and Indian War.

Marshall obviously did get a regular commission after
graduating from Virginia Military Institute in 1901, but
people with the right political connections had to exert a
fair amount of energy to accomplish it. He too had his share
of disappointments in a small, peacetime army. Once at
least he considered resignation in favor of the business
world. Through no fault of his own, it took him fifteen years
to make captain and a total of thirty-four years to reach
brigadier general. Washington and Marshall were very ambitious men, but they were also determined and persistent.
Neither knew the meaning of failure. If Washington was an
ideal man to lead a revolution, Marshall had the stamina
and tenacity to direct a worldwide military effort nearly two
centuries later. Both of these hard-driving soldiers found
diversion and relaxation in riding and hunting, an ancient
Virginia pastime.

A second professional comparison concerns the importance of World War I for Marshall and of the French and
Indian War for Washington. Marshall, involved with planning for many thousands of men in a multiplicity of ways,
tucked away lessons to be acted on two decades later. What
may be less clear is the relationship between Washington's

experiences in the 1750s and his service on the larger stage that was the War of Independence. It will be recalled, however, that not only did Washington command a regiment as a colonial, but during the Forbes campaign he also headed a considerably larger body, an advance division; here he gained the professional respect of both field-grade and general officers in the British service, including Thomas Gage, Edward Braddock, William Shirley, John Stanwix, Henry Bouquet, John Forbes, and Robert Monckton.

From their background and training, both Washington and Marshall had learned how to challenge men to give their best. They did so not by pompous rhetoric or theatrics but in part at least by the example of their own labor and dedication. It is common knowledge that Marshall always had to battle the tendency to be a workaholic; so too did Washington, whose eight-and-a-half years as commander of the Continental forces without a leave of absence surely must be some sort of record in the annals of our military history. Both encouraged subordinates to be independent and creative, traits not invariably appreciated by those of the highest civilian or military station. Some authorities, feeling threatened by bright juniors, only give lip service to qualities of candor and openness. Washington and Marshall did not surround themselves with sycophants. They were intelligent, though not remarkably imaginative or flashy with their mental endowments; they wanted to be challenged, they asked questions, and they were good listeners.

While Washington drew upon Greene, Knox, and Steuben, Marshall had his Arnold, Bradley, Eisenhower, and Clark. General Henry H. "Hap" Arnold, Army Air Corps chief, remembered that at the outset Chief of Staff Marshall lacked a full appreciation of airpower but that he learned quickly and was open-minded, part of "his ability to digest what he saw" and incorporate it into his "body of military genius."[15] General Omar Bradley recalled a revealing occurrence that took place soon after he joined the secretariat of the new chief of staff in 1939: "At the end of the first week General Marshall called us into his office and said without ceremony, 'I am disappointed in all of you.' When we asked why, he replied, 'You haven't disagreed with a single thing I have done all week.' " Later, when Bradley and his colleagues questioned the contents of a staff study, Marshall said approvingly, "Now that is what I want. Unless I hear all the arguments against something I am not sure whether I've made the right decision or not." And to Eisenhower, before the North African landings, Marshall declared, "When you disagree with my point of view, say so, without an apologetic approach."[16]

If it is not clear how Washington came by such qualities, it appears probable that Marshall was significantly influenced by his mentor, General Pershing. On various occasions in later years Marshall mentioned approvingly Pershing's remarkable capacity to accept dissent. As Marshall informed Colonel Edwin T. Cole in 1939, Pershing "could listen to more opposition to his apparent view than any man I have ever known, and show less personal feeling than anyone I have ever seen. He was the most outstanding example of a man with complete tolerance regardless of what his own personal opinions seemed to be. In that quality lay a great part of his strength."[17]

Washington's and Marshall's quiet, low-key, reflective manner of instilling confidence and bestowing recognition contrasted sharply with that of certain other military chieftains—Leonard Wood, for example, whose charm and way of inspiring subordinates is captured in a story by Frederick Palmer, a war correspondent in Cuba. Emerging from Wood's tent, a young officer exclaimed, "I have just met the greatest man in the world, and I'm the second greatest."[18] The illustration is not meant to imply that one method was right and another wrong but rather to indicate that a general must resort to methods of leadership compatible with his own persona. Actually, Washington and Marshall were by natural disposition inclined to be fiery and temperamental, but they had subdued these inherent tendencies by mastering self-control. There were exceptions; neither suffered fools easily. There are tales of Washington swearing so mightily as to shake leaves from trees and of Marshall's blistering tongue peeling paint from walls.[19]

For the most part, however, Marshall, like Washington, had sufficient patience to be recognized as an excellent teacher, and it goes without saying that no military arm can be fully professional without superior teaching. While Washington was never an instructor in a formal sense, he urged the creation of a military academy—a step delayed until Jefferson's presidency. Marshall, who taught and occasionally lectured at a number of military institutions, has been particularly praised for his positive impact on the officer students and junior instructors at the Infantry School; during his five years there as deputy commandant he dealt with two hundred future World War II generals, including Bradley, Collins, Ridgway, Stillwell, and Van Fleet. As early as 1937, before it was clear that Marshall would vault the seniority obstacle and make it to the top rung of the military ladder, there were officers—so Marshall learned from Lieutenant Colonel John F. Landis—"who regard[ed] themselves as self-appointed 'Marshall men'."[20]

Both Washington and Marshall were attuned to the relationship between subject matter and pupil at all levels of instruction. American servicemen were not simply soldiers; they were American soldiers, products of a free and open society, where restraints upon individual action and expression were minimal compared to many other parts of the world. That fact could be frustrating, but it could also offer dividends. Marshall and Washington were in agreement that Americans possessed the substance to be first-rate

fighting men. That meant, however, that they must know
the issues involved and must recognize that their officers
were sensitive to their well-being. "Soldiers will tolerate almost anything in an officer except unfairness and ignorance," stated Marshall. "They are quick to detect either."
Marshall scholars have put such emphasis on this aspect of
the general's military thought that it hardly requires further
elaboration.[21]

The teaching point enables us to form a transitional link
between our two generals as professionals on the one hand
and as military leaders mindful of domestic and political
factors on the other. They deserve to be remembered as professionals, albeit not in a narrow Huntingtonian sense.
They were not greatly troubled by the nation's alleged anti-
militarism, by the fear that civilian attitudes and values
made genuine professionalism all but impossible in America—that is to say, out of the question unless the army could
remain distant from what some officers saw as corrupting
and undermining civilian influences. Undeniably Washington fussed and fumed during the Revolution about certain civilian attitudes and practices. He also lamented the
lack of long-term enlistments and the inadequacies of green
militia; but these remarks, so often quoted by Emory Upton
and other adovcates of a modified Prussian military system
for America, were uttered in the midst of a stressful war
that he was in danger of losing.

It is most revealing to see what Commander in Chief
Washington and Chief of Staff Marshall thought about the
future peacetime military picture for the country. At the request of the Continental Congress in 1783, Washington prepared a lengthy document entitled "Sentiments on a Peace
Establishment."[22] He expressed his preference for a small
yet highly trained professional army with a federally organized state militia system as a reserve force, a system he
considered realistic as to American resources and values.

Washington's plan was praised by a career officer and prolific writer, John McAuley Palmer, as the best scheme of
national defense ever proposed, one far superior to Upton's
far-fetched pleas and one that Palmer's friend George C.
Marshall also found in keeping with American principles.
As early as the immediate post–World War I years and before Palmer had "discovered" Washington's long-neglected
"Sentiments," the two friends—veterans of years of service
but still relative juniors because of the army's complex promotion mills—felt that a substantial army for the 1920s
would be unhealthy for the country.

Marshall encouraged Palmer in his determination to
write a book that would draw attention to Washington's
"Sentiments," and he gave Palmer's manuscript a careful
reading before it was published in 1930. Washington, who
had only negative value for the Uptonians, now became the
champion of all those favoring the concept of a nation in
arms, of whom Palmer was the most persistent and elo-
quent spokesman over several decades.[23]

Palmer was at pains to point out that Upton's views on
Washington and militia were inadequate, that Washington
had actually made a crucial distinction between untrained
irregulars (who usually, but not always, performed dismally
in the Revolution) and militia who received systematic instruction under federal guidelines, as he advocated in his
"Sentiments" and later during his presidency. Palmer also
observed that Washington commented approvingly on the
well-structured Swiss militia of the eighteenth century;
Palmer felt the Swiss citizen-army of nearly two hundred
years later was equally worthy of American attention.

While Palmer was the first military writer to cast important light on Washington's thinking about the defense of the
nation—the political (or "Ike") dimensions of his military
thought, Palmer tended to slight the Virginian's contributions to army professionalism. Those thoughts, too, were

present in his "Sentiments" and in his state papers as president. Washington advocated a highly proficient army that included artillerists, engineers, and officers educated at a national military academy.

If Marshall seems to have held a more balanced view than Palmer about the relationship between professionals and citizen-soldiers, he nonetheless continued to share certain of Palmer's concerns about a bloated professional establishment; he had far more in common with his old friend than with the Uptonians. Interestingly, Marshall himself resorted to a pejorative expression, dating from early American whiggery and Jeffersonian Republicanism, in his final report as chief of staff in 1945. "There must not be," he warned, "a large standing army subject to the behest of schemers. The citizen-soldier is the guarantee against such a misuse of power." According to Marshall, military needs should not be determined in a vacuum, should not be approached as military needs and nothing more. Rather, one must ask whether they would burden the country economically and whether they were compatible with American principles, as Washington himself had said in advising against a sizable regular presence in 1783.[24]

Even so, neither Washington in 1783 nor Marshall in 1945 prevailed in his recommendations for postwar national defense. Like Washington, Marshall recommended universal military training, and in so doing he invoked the name and wisdom of the first commander in chief. Aware of the delicacy of the issue, both Washington and Marshall had stressed a time limit for military *training* rather than requesting extended military *service* with a small professional army, however small or republican in character that army might be. Responding enthusiastically to Marshall's report, Palmer exclaimed that Marshall had "translated Washington's philosophy into the language and thought of the atomic age."[25]

A complexity of factors accounts for the country's rejection of peacetime compulsory training, both in 1783 and in 1945. For better or worse, Americans have been ill-disposed to reflect seriously about their future security following a victorious war. Yet a fundamental question of concern to Washington and Marshall—namely, the citizen's obligation to the country's defense—was itself well within the limits of proper national discussion.

The decade of the 1980s opened with yet another debate involving American security requirements; it included controversies over conscription versus volunteer forces, over the nature of an adequate nuclear shield, and, more broadly, over domestic versus military priorities. Marshall's words about a well-informed citizenry, quoted in the last chapter, were never more pertinent. In short, Marshall believed that defense spending was so expensive and freighted with so many far-reaching implications that the public could not leave the subject solely to the experts, who themselves often disagreed. Nor, for that matter, was there usually a consensus among the military itself (witness the sharp clashes since the 1920s between Uptonians and Palmerians) or among civilians responsible for formulating defense policy. Marshall was as acutely attuned as Washington to the relationship between the home front and battle front. What I. B. Holley, Jr. has said of Palmer may be said equally of Marshall: "He understood . . . that the manpower of the nation should never be mobilized without first mobilizing the national will. The humiliating disaster in Vietnam stands as compelling evidence of the national failure to grasp this insight which suffused Palmer's thinking."[26]

Neither Washington nor Marshall was enamored of war. If conflict had possessed a glamorous appeal in previous ages, asserted Marshall, it was no longer so in the twentieth century. Washington as president was accused of cowardly behavior in his determination to avoid hostilities in the face of British aggressions on the high seas and in the North-west. Marshall, speaking before the American Historical Association, charged his scholarly audience with the task of investigating seriously the "deadly disease" of war, of which "a complete knowledge" was "essential before we can hope to find a cure." In a modest way, the army itself might make a contribution to the study of war through the Historical Section of the War College. Marshall, however, did not share the view of General Pershing in the 1920s that the Historical Section should issue critical replies to historians who found fault with various aspects of the American military performance during World War I. Colonel Oliver L. Spaulding, chief of the Historical Section, proposed that the adjutant general extend a written offer to every state superintendent of public instruction to have military men review American history textbooks "as to the accuracy of their presentation of facts." Marshall advised Pershing that many education leaders would interpret such a campaign as an attempt "to mould public opinion along militaristic lines." Besides, "once a book has been printed, its author and publisher would undoubtedly actively resent unfavorable reviews by the War Department." Fortunately, Marshall's wise counsel prevailed.[27]

Given their deep understanding of American history and culture, Washington and Marshall seem obvious choices for T. Harry Williams's category of "Ike"-type military leaders. Why then did Williams leave them out? We can only speculate; perhaps he omitted them because they were not the affable, easygoing sort that Williams associated with his definition of the "Ikes." But does one have to be friendly and folksy to recognize that officers would lead wartime armies composed of citizen-soldiers, to appreciate the problems of civilian leadership, and to work harmoniously with that leadership? The careers of Washington and Marshall allow us to answer that question with a decided "no." If blessed with wisdom and integrity, the man who holds him-self back a bit may command great respect; and it is quite plausible to maintain that both men used their natural reserve to good effect. "Familiarity breeds contempt," is the saying; not "Reserve elicits disrespect."

It is not enought for us to say that the "Ikes", along with Washington and Marshall, believed in civil supremacy, for undoubtedly the "Mac" generals themselves were dedicated to American constitutional government. Even so, as Williams notes, the story of the "Macs" should make us mindful that civil-military relations have not always been so tranquil as we might like to think. McClellan grew up on Jomini, who said that after wars commenced the civilian authorities should retire and let the soldiers manage the fighting without interference, a view rejected by President Lincoln. Nor, of course, did Truman accept the interpretation of civil-military relations in wartime expressed by MacArthur after his removal from his Far Eastern post in 1951. "A theatre commander," MacArthur stated, "is not merely limited to the handling of his troops; he commands the whole area, politically, economically and militarily. At that stage of the game when politics fails and the military takes over, you must trust the military. . . . When men become locked in battle there should be no artifice under the name of politics which should handicap your own men."[28]

Where then is the difference between the "Macs" on the one hand and the "Ikes" and Washington and Marshall on the other, so far as civil control is concerned? The latter not only believed in it, as did the "Macs," but they *understood* it as well, in all its dimensions. Civil control meant, among other things, that the central government could not always give first priority to the military's total needs as defined by the military, because of homefront requirements, or political considerations, or international factors. Time and again Washington endeavored to explain this truth to his discontented officers and men during the War of Independence. Furthermore, as Marshall said during World War II, democracies inevitably go to war ill prepared and they do not conduct their conflicts very efficiently. He later added that "tolerance and understanding of our democratic procedures and reactions are very necessary" for military men. If Washington felt political pressures in the Revolution to hold New York City and defend Philadelphia, the patriots' capital, Marshall made a point of telling various classes at military schools that for reasons of home-front morale the politicians insisted on some major offensive thrust each year, beginning in 1942.[29]

Washington and Marshall not only adjusted to the realities of war in a free society but were also praised for doing so. Both were extolled to an almost unhealthy degree in a nation that has always been uncertain in its thinking about soldiers and military institutions. It troubled John Adams and his cousin Samuel that Washington was deified by his admirers. It did not disturb Presidents Roosevelt and Truman to speak of Marshall as the indispensable man.

Although our two army chiefs never succumbed to a Narcissus complex, they were not hesitant to speak out against actions and policies they considered ill advised; upon assuming the top army post in 1939, Marshall went so far as to warn Roosevelt that he would speak forthrightly. Here in the nature of their occasional dissent from governmental decisions was a part of the American military tradition worth preserving. To be loyal is not always to be silent. The crucial question is how to go about it, for in this case a thin line may at times separate right from wrong. Still, it should be permissible, even desirable, for the military man to speak up if he feels that policies are plainly in error or in need of revision, provided he does so without endeavoring to create executive-legislative friction or without undermining the political and constitutional system. One wonders to what extent the Truman-MacArthur controversy subsequently inhibited the "top brass" from speaking their minds either for or against greater military involvement in a given situation. General William C. Westmoreland, American commander in Vietnam, recalled that President Lyndon B. Johnson remarked just before a televised press conference, "I hope you don't pull a MacArthur on me."[30]

Certainly there are risks involved in dissent or expressions of unorthodoxy, particularly if the general or admiral is perceived as being indiscreet; he may get into hot water with the administration in Washington, with the public, or with both. In some respects, problems of this nature plagued a number of senior officers: General Leonard Wood, army chief of staff before America's entrance into World War I; General Billy Mitchell, an irrepressible evangelist for air power in the 1920s; Admiral Arthur W. Radford, chairman of the joint chiefs of staff under Eisenhower in the 1950s, who was accused of being enamored of nuclear weapons; and General Curtis E. LeMay of the air force, whose comments on bombing in Southeast Asia were embarrassing to the national administration.[31]

Historically, military men in America have been quite sensitive to criticism, and Washington and Marshall were not exceptions; but at least they understood it as the inevitable result of our personal freedoms, and they were somewhat philosophical about it, as was a recent general, Omar N. Bradley, who greatly admired both Washington and Marshall. "If a soldier would command an army," cautioned the World War II commander and later chairman of the joint chiefs of staff, "he must be prepared to withstand those who would criticize the manner in which he leads that army. There is no place in a democratic state for the attitude that would elevate each military hero above public reproach simply because he did the job that he has been trained and paid to do."[32]

There was assuredly one kind of rebuke that Washington and Marshall never felt. They were not on the losing side of an extremely controversial war, as were American officers involved in the Vietnam conflict. Rightly or wrongly, some military leaders in that tragic endeavor suffered the sting of severe judgments. One such leader was General West-moreland, who sued the Columbia Broadcasting Company because of a television feature that raised disturbing questions about the possibility at the army's top levels of a conspiracy to alter and withhold intelligence in Vietnam. Drew Middleton, interviewing officers roughly a decade after the United States's troop withdrawal from Southeast Asia, concluded that many officers then entering the senior ranks complained of not having been given a freer hand in the 1960s. They were still rankled by memories of "the incomprehension of military realities on the part of the civilian leadership," including Presidents Kennedy, Johnson, and Nixon. As one officer confided to Middleton, the civilians had "no military background" that would help them "understand the situation." Westmoreland, who claimed no bitterness in *A Soldier Reports*, as well as no feeling that the military had been made a scapegoat for the outcome, nonetheless seemed to sympathize with the concerns that Middleton found. "Over-all control of the military is one thing; shackling professional military men with restrictions in professional matters imposed by civilians who lack military understanding is another."[33]

If some critics agreed with Westmoreland that civil control worked all too well, their explanation for it varied appreciably from the general's. They contended that the uniformed high command, both in our nation's capital and in Saigon, misunderstood the responsibilities attached to civil control. The service heads should have told their civilian lords bluntly that the government's objectives of maintaining (or creating?) a truly viable state in South Vietnam could not be realized in view of the restraints imposed upon American forces. While we normally like our senior officers to keep a low profile, according to this analysis the joint chiefs overdid it: intimidated by administration stalwarts, they backed plans they actually opposed or should have rejected. Although one or more of the generals or admirals might have resigned out of principle (and perhaps as a result brought pressure to bear for an honest, comprehensive policy review), none did so out of "loyalty." A further contention is that the military elite did not really wish to sound off; they were less frustrated than was claimed at a later time. They wished to let the civilians who took the country into that undeclared war live with the consequences. The military commanders elected to ignore or slight larger Clausewitzian questions involving national will and national priorities. They had, in the stern judgment of Paul M. Kattenburg, abdicated their "military-political responsibility in favor of single-minded concentration on the technocratic aspects of war."[34]

However much validity we attach to these and other interpretations of the military command's alleged shortcomings in the Vietnam War, it seems safe to say that the Washington-Marshall habit of constructive but loyal dissent did not assert itself forcefully in the Kennedy-Johnson-Nixon era; if it did, the evidence for it has scarcely been brought to light in convincing fashion. Yet the Washington and Marshall type of candor was revived by some active and retired military leaders in the early 1980s. For example, Generals David Jones, John A. Wickham, Jr., and Edward C. Meyer, all at one time or another members of the joint chiefs, uttered public statements about the political and strategic factors and circumstances they deemed prerequisite to American armed intervention anywhere in the world.

Transparently the American military, at least at the highest levels, was showing signs of being less defensive and sen-

sitive in the 1980s than a decade or so earlier—and with
good reason. Over the last two centuries the American military had suffered no more abuse than other sectors of government; since Vietnam, if not during the war itself, it had
suffered even less: less than the President, the Congress,
and the Supreme Court. Washington, for instance, received
far more slings and arrows as the chief executive than he
did as a general, and so did Taylor, Grant, and Eisenhower.
As for Marshall, his performance as a civilian in several
high-level posts in the Truman administration brought him
the most vicious kind of abuse—character assassination
and accusations of treason—from far right sectors in the
country.[35]

Whatever ills American military personnel feel are in-
flicted upon them from time to time, they can better understand and respond to their critics if they have had a healthy
diversity of experiences with the civilian sector of American
life. Such a background requires a uniting of the best of the
political (or "Ike") and the professional components of the
American military tradition. Washington and Marshall
demonstrate, in their military careers, that a union of these
components is both possible and desirable. Huntington's
brand of narrow professionalism seems less appealing in the
1980s than it did in the 1950s when *The Soldier and the State*
appeared and received high praise in and out of the armed
services.

Many officers never reached full career maturity in the
sort of physical and intellectual isolation that was once
claimed to breed the finest kind of professionalism. Even in
the Sherman era, the commanding general himself put officers to work with the National Guard and dispatched
them to training camps. He referred to the employment of
the army to break up labor disorders—a common use of
troops in the Gilded Age—as "beneath a soldier's voca-
tion," and he spoke disparagingly of expansion into Canada

and the West Indies ("We want no more territory"). Nelson A. Miles, a commanding general from 1894 to 1903, also extended the military's influence into the civilian community; he displayed a special interest in assigning officers to teach military science in private and public colleges. Miles too had a keen interest in American values, which influenced his military thinking. He stated privately that President William McKinley had launched a "political war" against Spain in 1898. He considered American imperialism a violation of the principles of the American Revolution. In retirement he castigated the Second Cuban Intervention not only on moral grounds but also on grounds that America would find "to[o] big a job" were she to become "the police of the world."[36]

In all likelihood, meaningful interaction with civilian society must begin relatively early if the officer is to appreciate later on the broad range of matters that should legitimately concern military higher-ups. The demands are enormous, for they involve the relationship between military strategy and national policy, and they must not neglect natural resources, scientific developments, public opinion, domestic politics, as well as many other concerns. Washington repeatedly acknowledged implicitly what Marshall stated specifically: that it had been necessary (in his case, for the joint chiefs during World War II) to devote "more time in our discussions, our intimate discussions," to political "matters [than] to any [other] subject." Dean Acheson concurred: when Marshall "thought about military problems, non military factors played a controlling part."[37]

Washington as a young officer on the frontier had to deal with townspeople and farmers, with militiamen and volunteers, and with Virginia's executive and legislative politicians—all prior to his many years as a lawmaker, first in the House of Burgesses and then in the Continental Congress. As for Marshall, his remarkable insights into civilian attitudes and values owed much to his frequent teaching assignments with the National Guard over a period of thirty years. From an early stage in his career, he was acknowledged by professionals and amateurs alike as singularly proficient in dealing with guardsmen, whom he felt must be accorded more than customary courtesy. When in 1908 the War Department established a Division of Militia Affairs to provide greater control over the National Guard, General Franklin Bell tried and failed to get Marshall appointed assistant to the division head, a compliment nonetheless to the twenty-eight-year-old lieutenant.

Without doubt, some officers have had ample exposure to the civilian community and still fallen short in the area of civil-military relations. Probably a partial explanation for those failures lies in the fundamental character of the officers concerned. Experience alone does not guarantee future achievement, but it assuredly helps—particularly if the experience comes at a formative stage in an officer's career, and if he has the opportunity to build on that experience as did Marshall. He gained further insight into the civilian realm by accompanying Chief of Staff Pershing to congressional hearings, interacting with the academic world through participation at R.O.T.C. conferences, seeking opportunities to speak to civic and business clubs and organizations, and working with the New Deal's Civilian Conservation Corps in the 1930s. All these activities narrow-minded officers would have scorned as digressions from military professionalism.

Marshall realized at the time that they were invaluable. In 1938, he declared that his recent three-year assignment "with the Illinois National Guard [w]as one of the most instructive and valuable military experiences I have had." Judging from Marshall's own assessments, his several assignments that involved the establishment and administration of CCC programs were equally beneficial. They constituted "the most interesting problem of my Army career," he told Pershing in 1933. Five years later his opinion had not changed. "I found the CCC the most instructive service I have ever had, and the most interesting," he observed to General George Grunert.[38]

What had he learned? From his years with the National Guard and the CCC Marshall gained know-how in the mobilization, organization, and administration of large bodies of civilians. This proved to be crucial training for the man later entrusted as chief of staff with the responsibility of preparing millions of draftees for duty in World War II. For the time being, until the draftees were ready for action, the military force that would separate America from disaster would be the National Guard. Marshall believed that America would no longer have the luxury, as in World War I, of waiting months before making a heavy human commitment. "We must be prepared the next time we are involved in war, to fight immediately, that is within a few weeks, somewhere and somehow," he advised in March 1939. "Now that means we will have to employ the National Guard for that purpose, because it will constitute the large majority of the war army of the first six months." Yet, complained Marshall, too much of current American military training implied that the nation would begin to fight with combat-ready professionals; at Fort Leavenworth, for instance, he stated that the faculty could not see the forest for the trees.[39]

Consequently, Marshall believed that upgrading the National Guard was vital. Its training would afford the miniscule peacetime army practical awareness of the art it must have when conflict erupted. It would also bolster America's defenses and provide the nucleus of the citizen army that would ultimately fight a future war (which Marshall foresaw as coming). Citizen forces had been the military backbone of the country in all its previous armed struggles.

No officers have ever equalled Washington and Marshall in effectively bridging the gap between the civilian and the military. To state the matter differently, in terms recalling the theories of Williams and Huntington, Washington and Marshall united the best of both the professional and the political (or "Ike") characteristics of the American military tradition. *Time* said of Marshall: "In a general's uniform, he stood for the civilian substance of this democratic society." Pogue tells us that Marshall "became familiar with the civilian point of view in a way rare among professional military men." A staff member remarked that "Marshall had a feeling for civilians that few Army officers . . . have had. . . . He didn't have to adjust to civilians—they were a natural part of his environment. . . . I think he regarded civilians and military as part of a whole." Washington said it even better: "We should all be considered Congress, Army, &c. as one people, embarked in one Cause, in one interest; acting on the same principle and to the same End."[40]

Notes

Introduction

1. Daniel R. Hundley, *Social Relations in Our Southern States* (New York, 1860), 49–50.

2. Willard Thorp, *A Southern Reader* (New York, 1955), 287–88. Other writers who speculate on various aspects of Southern martial behavior include John Hope Franklin, *The Militant South, 1800–1861* (New York, 1956); Marcus Cunliffe, *Soldiers and Civilians: The Martial Spirit in America, 1775–1865* (New York, 1968), chap. 10; Bertram Wyatt-Brown, *Southern Honor: Ethics and Behavior in the Old South* (New York, 1982); Grady Mc-Whinney and Perry D. Jamieson, *Attack and Die: Civil War Military Tactics and the Southern Heritage* (University, Ala., 1982).

3. George W. Corner, ed., *Autobiography of Benjamin Rush* (Philadelphia, 1948), 112–13.

4. W. W. Abbot et al., eds., *Papers of George Washington: Colonial Series*, 4 vols. to date (Charlottesville, 1983–), 4:90 (hereafter cited as *Papers of Washington*).

5. Quoted in A. B. Hart, ed., *Commonwealth History of Massachusetts*, 5 vols. (New York, 1927–1930), 2:461.

6. John Adams to Nathanael Greene, August 4, 1776, *Papers of Nathanael Greene*, ed. Richard K. Showman et al., 3 vols. to date (Chapel Hill, 1976–), 1:273.

7. Charles Royster, *A Revolutionary People at War: The Continental Army and the American Character, 1775–1783* (Chapel Hill, 1979), chap. 1.

ONE
The Colonial Tradition

1. Douglas S. Freeman, *George Washington: A Biography*, 7 vols. (New York, 1948–1957), 3:292. Freeman's associates, John A. Carroll and Mary W. Ashworth, wrote the final volume following his death.

2. *Papers of Washington*, 1:336; "The Journal of Captain Robert Cholmley's Batman," in *Braddock's Defeat*, ed. Charles Hamilton, (Norman,
Okla., 1959), 29. Washington recorded accounts of Braddock's disaster in
letters to Mary Ball Washington, to Robert Dinwiddie, to John Augustine Washington, all dated July 18, 1755, in *Papers of Washington*,
1:336–45. For Washington's later reflections, see "Biographical Memoranda," October 1783, in *Writings of George Washington. . . .* ed. John C.
Fitzpatrick, 39 vols. (Washington, D.C., 1931–1944), 29:42–45 (hereafter cited as *Writings of Washington*).

3. *Papers of Washington*, 1:336, 339. Captain Cholmley's servant would
seem to confirm Washington's view of the provincials. He declared, "I
believe their might be two hundred of the American Soldiers that fought
behind Trees and I believe they did the moast Execution of Any." "Journal of Captain Robert Cholmley's Batman," *Braddock's Defeat*, ed. Hamilton, 29. See fuller praise of the Virginians in Joseph Ball to Washington,
September 5, 1755, *Papers of Washington*, 2:15.

4. John Bolling to Robert Bolling, August 13, 1755, quoted in *Papers of
Washington*, 2 n. 1. For reference to "our Brave Blues," see John Martin to
Washington, August 30, 1755, ibid., 11.

5. Thomas Nairne, "A Letter from a Swiss Gentleman to his Friend in
Bern," *North Carolina University Magazine* 4 (1855), 297.

6. *Boston Gazette*, September 19, 1755; *Boston Weekly News-Letter*, August
21, 1755; Charles Chauncy, *A Letter to a Friend, Giving a Concise, but Just
Account . . . Of the Ohio-Defeat* (Boston, 1755), 7–8.

7. Douglas E. Leach, *Arms for Empire: A Military History of the British
Colonies in North America, 1607–1763* (New York, 1973), 507.

8. *Boston Evening Post*, December 6, 1773. While in England, Franklin
in February 1775 published a letter in the *Public Advertiser* in which he
reminded his readers that colonial soldiers had "covered the Retreat of
the British Regulars and saved them from utter Destruction in the Expedition under Braddock" (Verner W. Crane, ed., *Benjamin Franklin's Letters
to the Press, 1758–1775* [Chapel Hill, 1950], 279–82).

9. Quoted in John E. Ferling, *A Wilderness of Miseries: War and Warriors
in Early America* (Westport, Conn., 1980), 16. Washington's superior, Governor Robert Dinwiddie, would have scarcely disagreed. "On my arrival
at my Gov't, I found the Militia in very bad Order," he informed the
Board of Trade (February 24, 1756, *The Official Records of Robert Dinwiddie . . . 1752–1758*, ed. R. A. Brock, 2 vols. [Richmond, 1883–1884],
1:344). A decade or so earlier, an English visitor wrote of the Virginia
militia: "alas! to behold the Musters of their Militia, would induce a
Man to Nauseate a Sash and hold a Sword forever in Derision. Diversity

of Weapons and Dresses, Unsizeableness of the Men, and Want of the least Grain of Discipline in their Officers or them, make the whole Scene little better than Dryden has expressed it. . . . : And raw in fields the rude militia swarms; . . . Of seeming arms, they make a short essay, then hasten so get drunk the bus'ness of the day" ("Observations in Several Voyages and Travels in America," reprinted from the *London Magazine* for July 1744, *William and Mary Quarterly*, 1st series, 15 [1907], 147–48).

10. For the raising of provincials for the Cartagena expedition, see H. C. McBarron et al., "The American Regiment, 1740–1746," *Military Collector and Historian* 21 (1969), 84–86. For the companies of Virginians serving with Braddock, see Dinwiddie to Thomas Robinson, March 17, 1755, *Dinwiddie Papers*, ed. Brock, 1:525; Franklin T. Nichols, "The Organization of Braddock's Army," *William and Mary Quarterly*, 3d series, 4 (1947), 130–33.

11. "Commission," August 14, 1755, *Papers of Washington* 2:3–4.

12. References to Washington's enthusiasm for military service are in *Papers of Washington* 1:226, 278, 243. Freeman, *Washington* 1:77, on Lawrence Washington. As Douglas Leach says, "Cartagena soon became a tradition in the American colonies, and those who had been there and returned were looked upon as heroes" (*Arms for Empire*, 218). Washington's description of Fort James is in Donald Jackson and Dorothy Twohig, eds., *The Diaries of George Washington*, 6 vols. (Charlottesville, 1976–1979), 1:36, 75; Freeman, *Washington* 1:250–51. Washington's friend and mentor William Fairfax subsequently assured him that his familiarity with the writings of military authors should enable him to bear up better under the burdens of command (Fairfax to Washington, May 13–14, 1756, *Papers of Washington* 3:125).

13. Ibid., 1:348 n. 7; *Writings of Washington* 29:45. For Washington's opinion of Braddock during the campaign, see his letters to John Augustine Washington, May 6, 1755, and to William Fairfax, June 7, 1755, *Papers of Washington* 1:266–67, 298–300. Washington's fencing is mentioned in Freeman, *Washington* 2:204.

14. "Orders," January 8, 1756, *Papers of Washington* 2:257.

15. Ibid.

16. "Orders," October 26, 1755, *Papers of Washington* 2:136.

17. "General Instructions to all the Captains of Companies," July 29, 1757, *Papers of Washington* 4:341–45. As to his differences with Braddock, Washington wrote: "The General, by frequent breaches of Contracts, has lost all degree of Patience; and for want of that consideration, & moderation which should be used by a Man of Sense upon these occasions, will, I fear, represent us home in a light we little deserve; for instead of blame-

ing the Individuals as he ought, he charges all his Disappointments to publick Supineness; and looks upon the Country, I believe, as void of both Honour and Honesty; we have frequent dispu[tes] on this head, which are maintained with warmth on both sides especially on his, who is incapable of Arguing witht; or giving up any points he asserts, let it be ever so incompatible with Reason." Washington to William Fairfax, June 7, 1755, *Papers of Washington* 1:298–99. The fullest account of British difficulties concerning quartering, impressment, and recruitment is Alan Rogers, *Empire and Liberty: American Resistance to British Authority, 1755–1763* (Berkeley, 1974), chaps. 4, 5, 7.

18. Stanley M. Pargellis, "Braddock's Defeat," *American Historical Review* 41 (1936), 253–69; Lee McCardell, *Ill-Starred General: Braddock of the Coldstream Guards* (Pittsburgh, 1958), chap. 12, especially p. 229; Paul E. Kopperman, *Braddock at the Monongahela* (Pittsburgh, 1977), 13–14, 16–17; John Shy, *Toward Lexington: The Role of the British Army in the Coming of the American Revolution* (Princeton, 1965), 127; Lawrence H. Gipson, *The British Empire before the American Revolution*, 15 vols. (Caldwell, Idaho and New York, 1936–1970), 6:86, 94. British flexible responses in both Europe and America are discussed in Peter E. Russell, "Redcoats in the Wilderness: British Officers and Irregular Warfare in Europe and America, 1740–1760," *William and Mary Quarterly*, 3d Series, 34 (1978), 629–52. Early American warfare is also accurately placed within the context of military developments in the Western World in two essays by Peter Paret: "Colonial Experience and European Military Reform at the End of the Eighteenth Century," *Bulletin of the Institute of Historical Research* 37 (1964), 49–56; "The Relationship between the Revolutionary War and European Military Thought and Practice in the Second Half of the Eighteenth Century," in *Reconsiderations on the Revolutionary War*, ed. Don Higginbotham (Westport, Conn., 1978), 144–57.

19. *Papers of Washington* 2:257, 23, 4:344; J. A. Houlding, *Fit for Service: The Training of the British Army, 1715–1795* (Oxford, 1981), 195–99 passim.

20. *Papers of Washington* 4:344, 343, 2:76, 124, 135.

21. "Biographical Memoranda," October 1783, *Writings of Washington* 29:37; Washington to Dinwiddie, April 16, 1756, Stephen to Washington, March 29, 1756, *Papers of Washington* 3:1–2, 2:325.

22. William H. Browne, ed., *Correspondence of Governor Horatio Sharpe*, 3 vols. (Baltimore, 1888–1895), 1:416.

23. Washington to Dinwiddie, March 10, 1757, Memorial to Lord Loudoun, March 23, 1757, *Papers of Washington* 4:112–14, 120–21.

24. Freeman, *Washington* 2:407–8; William Henry Fairfax to Washington, December 9, 1757, *Letters to Washington*, ed. Stanislaus M. Hamilton, 5 vols. (Boston and New York, 1892–1902), 2:252–54; William Fair-

fax to Washington, July 17, 1757, *Papers of Washington* 4:309–10, 310–11 n. 3.

25. Freeman, *Washington* 2:204; Washington to Robinson, August 5, 1756, Washington to Dinwiddie, October 11, 1755, *Papers of Washington* 3:330, 2:102.

26. *Dinwiddie Papers* 2:425, 345, 346. For the fluctuations in Washington's troop strength and the reduction in number of frontier posts, see Bernhard Knollenberg, *George Washington: The Virginia Period, 1732–1775* (Durham, N.C., 1964), chaps. 7, 9, and especially notes, which are a mine of statistical information. See also "Return of the Virginia Regiment," October 9, 1756, January 1, 1757, *Papers of Washington* 3:428–29, 4:76–77.

27. "Memorandum respecting the Militia," May 9, 10, 1756, *Papers of Washington* 3:106, 111. As for a later turnout from Culpeper: "Out of the hundred that were draughted, seventy-odd arrived here; of which only twenty-five were tolerably armed." Washington to Dinwiddie, May 27, 1757, ibid., 4:264. According to Dinwiddie, "the Militia are not above one-half arm'd, and their Small Arms of different Bores making it very inconvenient in time of Action" (To the Board of Trade, February 24, 1756, *Dinwiddie Papers* 2:344).

28. *Papers of Washington* 3:432, 4:1–2, 12–13, 1:289; Freeman, *Washington* 2:216, 257–58; *Dinwiddie Papers* 1:387.

29. *Papers of Washington* 1:192 n. 3, 2:172, 174 n. 6, 3:66, 145–46; Freeman, *Washington* 2:189.

30. "Memorandum respecting the Militia," May 8, 1756, *Papers of Washington* 3:99.

31. Washington to Dinwiddie, November 9, 1756, ibid., 4:2. See also Washington to Robinson, November 9, 1756, ibid., 11–13.

32. W. W. Hening, ed., *The Statutes at Large: Being a Collection of All the Laws of Virginia from the First Session of the Legislature in the Year 1619*, 13 vols., (New York, Philadelphia, and Richmond, 1819–1823), 7:70–71; *Papers of Washington* 1:73. It is hazardous to generalize about the Virginia militia laws, which might be changed once or twice a year. Freeman, *Washington* 1:30 n. 21, discusses the statutes in force at the beginning of the French and Indian War. See also Shy, *A People Numerous and Armed*, 30. A number of the statutes are described in Richard L. Morton, *Colonial Virginia*, 2 vols. (Chapel Hill, 1960), vol. 2, chaps. 20–23.

33. Washington to Loudoun, January 10, 1757, *Papers of Washington* 4:79–80; Ann Maury, ed. and trans., *Memoirs of a Hugenot Family: Translated and Compiled from the Original Autobiography of the Reverend James Maury* (New York, 1833; reprinted Baltimore, 1967), 404.

This paragraph in the text draws on an important new study that was unknown to me until after I initially wrote this chapter: James W. Titus, "Soldiers When They Chose to be So: Virginians at War, 1754–1763" (Ph.D. diss., Rutgers University, 1983), particularly chap. 1. Titus also suggests that the use of the disadvantaged and disfranchised proved attractive, because it would preserve the harmonious relationship that existed between the colony's elites and its "middling" social orders. Besides, he notes, the government lacked the police power to carry out effectively what would have been the extremely controversial step of largescale mobilization of the yeomen-planter militia (Ibid., 111, 147–51).

34. Washington to Stanwix, April 10, 1758, Washington to Gage, April 12, 1758, *Writings of Washington* 2:173, 177.

35. Forbes to Pitt, September 6, 1758, *Writings of General John Forbes*, ed. A. P. James (Menasha, Wis., 1938), 205; Washington to Forbes, October 8, 1758, *Writings of Washington* 2:295–98.

36. Freeman, *Washington* 2:313.

37. "The Humble Address of the Officers of the Virginia Regiment," *Letters to Washington* 3:143–46. For other expressions of the officers' opinion of Washington, see *Theodorick Bland Papers*, 2 vols. (Richmond, 1840), 1:10; and various letters to Washington, particularly those of Adam Stephen, Hugh Mercer, and Robert Stewart in *Letters to Washington* and *Papers of Washington*. Consult as well Freeman, *Washington* 2:369–71.

38. Stewart to Washington, January 25, 1769, *Letters to Washington* 3:335. Dinwiddie's lament about the lack of experienced officers is in *Dinwiddie Papers* 1:94, 120. The attitudes of Forbes and his men toward the Virginians are described in Washington to Fauquier, September 25, 1758, *Writings of Washington* 2:290–91; Washington to George William Fairfax, September 25, 1758, "George Washington and the Fairfax Family: Some New Documents," ed. Peter Walne, *Virginia Magazine of History and Biography* 77 (1969), 455.

39. Samuel Davies, *Sermons on Important Subjects. . . . ,* 5 vols. (Philadelphia, 1818), 5:277, George W. Pelcher, *Samuel Davies: Apostle of Dissent in Colonial Virginia* (Knoxville, 1971), chap. 9, esp. 166–67.

40. Mercer to Washington, August 17, 1757, Stephen to Washington, August 20, 1757, *Papers of Washington* 4:372, 375.

41. Fred Anderson, "A People's Army: Provincial Military Service in Massachusetts during the Seven Years' War," *William and Mary Quarterly,* 3d series, 40 (1983), 500–27; Anderson, *A People's Army: Massachusetts Soldiers and Society in the Seven Years' War* (Chapel Hill, 1984), chap. 2.

42. Monckton to Amherst, July 9, 1760, quoted in Titus, "Soldiers When They Chose to be So," 243, 264 n. 69; Stewart to Washington, January 25, 1769, *Letters to Washington* 3:335.

43. For the Washington-Dinwiddie realtionship, see Knollenberg, *Washington,* chap. 9 and notes; Freeman, *Washington* 2:248, 260, 267, 270–75; John R. Alden, *Robert Dinwiddie: Servant of the Crown* (Charlottesville, 1973), 90–110.

44. Jack P. Greene, *The Quest for Power: The Lower Houses of Assembly in the Southern Royal Colonies, 1689–1776* (Chapel Hill, 1963), chap. 15, especially 303–6 for Dinwiddie's Virginia.

45. Washington to Robinson, December 19, 1756, *Papers of Washington* 4:68. While Councilor Fairfax was disposed to smooth things over (he had a good relationship with Dinwiddie), Speaker Robinson (who did not) seems to have encouraged such correspondence. See also Washington to Robinson, August 5, 1756, June 10, 1757, *Papers of Washington* 3:323–30, 4:198–99; Washington to Robinson, October 25, 1757, *Writings of Washington* 2:153–56; Fairfax to Washington, May 13–14, 1756, *Papers of Washington* 3:131.

46. Washington was particularly incensed by a September 3, 1756, essay, "The Virginia-Centennial No. X," in the *Virginia Gazette* (Hunter), that referred to some regimental officers as "dastardly Debauchees" who idled their time "skulking in Forts." Portions relating to the Virginia Regiment are quoted in *Papers of Washington* 3:410–11 n. 2. Washington himself, according to rumor, was thought by some in Williamsburg to have fabricated news of a likely Indian raid in the spring of 1757 in order to jolt the legislature into providing him with more men and necessaries. But Dinwiddie told Washington that he had not even heard the story until the colonel had brought it to his attention (Washington to Dinwiddie, September 17, 1757, Dinwiddie to Washington, September 24, 1757, ibid., 4:411–12, 422). The legislators raised various questions about regimental expenditures, including Washington's "extraordinary" idea that he needed both an aide and a secretary (William Fairfax to Washington, April 14, 1756, ibid., 2:351–52).

47. Washington to the earl of Loudoun, January 10, 1757, ibid., 4:79–90 (quotations, 83, 85).

48. Bland's eleven-page manuscript essay, signed "Philo patria," was endorsed by Washington, who evidently received a copy from the author: "Written it is supposed by Richard Bland Octo. 1756." The editors of the *Papers of Washington* note that the manuscript "is misfiled" in the Library of Congress's Washington collection "after the incoming letters of 1757" (3:437 n. 3). For Bland's continued support, see his letter to Washington, June 7, 1757, ibid., 4:187–88.

49. Kirkpatrick to Washington, June 19, 1757, *Papers of Washington* 4:237–38.

50. *Writings of Washington* 2:277–78, 278–83, 290–91, 294–95, 299–300 (quotation, 278); *Forbes Writings*, 199, 219.

TWO
Tradition in Transition

1. Washington to Fauquier, November 28, 1758, *The Official Papers of Francis Fauquier, Lieutenant Governor of Virginia, 1758–1768*, ed. George Reese, 3 vols. (Charlottesville, 1980–1983), 1:116. For the Washington-Fauquier letters, see ibid., 30–31, 35–36, 41–42, 50–52, 52–53, 57–58, 65–68, 72–73, 79–80, 81–82, 86–87, 96–97, 99–100, 104, 113, 117–18, 130–31, 171.

2. Freeman, *Washington* 3: 445.

3. Eliphalet Dyer of Connecticut, while alluding to sectional considerations in Washington's appointment and doubting that the Virginian had greater military credentials than some New Englanders, found Washington "a Gent. highly Esteemed by those acquainted with him." The new commander in chief seemed "discret & Virtuous, no harum Starum ranting Swearing fellow but Sober, steady, & Calm" (Dyer to Joseph Trumbull, June 17, 1775, *Letters of Delegates to Congress*, ed. Paul H. Smith et al., 10 vols. to date [Washington, D.C., 1976–], 1:499–500). Thomas Cushing of Massachusetts described Washington as "a complete gentleman. He is sensible, amiable, virtuous, modest, & brave. I promise myself that your acquaintance with him will afford you great pleasure, and I doubt not his agreeable behaviour & good conduct will give great satisfaction to our people of all denominations" (Cushing to James Bowdoin, Sr., June 21, 1775, ibid., 530). For further opinions of Washington that stress his personal character, see correspondence of John Adams, Silas Deane, and John Hancock, ibid., 497, 504, 506, 507, 517.

It may be no coincidence that the only other American general to be entrusted with a field army in the summer of 1775 was Philip Schuyler, who (like Washington) was at the time a member of Congress.

4. Gage to Washington, November 23, 1755, *Papers of Washington* 2:179.

5. Washington to Stephen, July 20, 1776, *Writings of Washington* 5:313.

6. Peter Force, ed., *American Archives . . .* , 4th series, 6 vols. (Washington, D.C., 1837–1846), 3:1077.

7. William Pencak, *War, Politics, and Revolution in Provincial Massachusetts* (Boston, 1981), xi, 154.

8. Ibid., 12. John Adams recalled much later that "the treatment of

the provincial officers and soldiers by the British officers during that war [French and Indian] made the blood boil in my veins" (Adams to Benjamin Rush, May 1, 1807, *The Spur of Fame: Dialogues of John Adams and Benjamin Rush, 1805–1813*, ed. John A. Schutz and Douglass Adair [San Marino, Calif., 1966], 82). Adams expressed similar opinions on other occasions. See C. F. Adams, ed., *The Works of John Adams*, 10 vols. (Boston, 1850–1856), 4:40, 9:611.

9. Robert J. Taylor, ed., *The Adams Papers: The Papers of John Adams*, 6 vols. to date (Cambridge, Mass., 1977–), 4:101; Massachusetts House of Representatives to Israel Mauduit, June 13, 1764, William Tudor, *Life of James Otis* (Boston, 1823), 166; Lyman H. Butterfield, ed., *The Adams Papers: Diary and Autobiography of John Adams*, 4 vols., (Cambridge, Mass., 1961), 1:285; James Otis, *The Rights of the British Colonies Asserted and Proved* (Boston, 1764), in *Pamphlets of the American Revolution, 1750–1776*, ed. Bernard Bailyn, 1 vol. to date (Cambridge, Mass., 1965–), 1:458–59, 463, 469; Jonathan Mayhew, *The Snare Broken* (Boston, 1766), 18–19; Samuel Adams to Christopher Gadsden, December 11, 1766, to Dennys De Berdt, December 16, 1766, *The Writings of Samuel Adams*, ed. Harry A. Cushing, 4 vols. (New York, 1904–1908), 1:110–11, 112–13.

10. *Writings of Washington* 3:305, 307–8.

11. *Boston Gazette*, May 21, 1754, quoted in Pencak, *War, Politics, and Revolution*, 233.

12. Julian P. Boyd et al., eds., *Papers of Thomas Jefferson*, 19 vols. to date (Princeton, 1950–), 2:195, 198 n. 1. For the revival of the militia, see Don Higginbotham, "The American Militia: A Traditional Institution with Revolutionary Responsibilities," in *Reconsiderations on the Revolutionary War*, ed. Higginbotham, 83–103 passim; John Todd White, "Standing Armies in Time of War: Republican Theory and Military Practice during the American Revolution" (Ph.D. diss., George Washington University, 1978), 86–111; Lawrence D. Cress, *Citizens in Arms: The Army and Militia in American Society* (Chapel Hill, 1982), 41–50.

13. John Adams to William Tudor, July 23, 26, 1775, to James Warren, July 23, 26, 1775, *Letters of Delegates to Congress* 1:650, 651–52, 667–68. One of John Adams's concerns was that Congress had initially given Washington power to appoint the heads of the quartermaster and commissary departments. Adams feared that a close relationship between Washington and high staff officers would prevent them from serving as a check on one another. For Gerry's and Adams's views of the militia, see James T. Austin, *Life of Elbridge Gerry*, 2 vols. (Boston, 1827–1828), 1:163, 176; George A. Billias, *Elbridge Gerry: Founding Father and Republican Statesman* (New York, 1976), 59–60.

14. Fred Anderson, "Why Did Colonial New Englanders Make Bad Soldiers? Contractual Principles and Military Conduct during the Seven Years' War," *William and Mary Quarterly*, 3d series, 38 (1981), 395–417 (quotation 401); Anderson, *A People's Army*, chap. 6.

15. The best treatment of the organization of the army is in Robert K. Wright, Jr., *The Continental Army* (Washington, D.C., 1983), which deals extensively with the formative months at Cambridge and with administrative and structural changes that occurred during the following years.

16. Gage to Washington, May 10, 1756, *Papers of Washington* 3:115; Washington to Joseph Reed, December 15, 1775, *Writings of Washington* 4:164–65; *The Fitch Papers* (Connecticut Historical Society, *Collections*, vols. 17–18 [1918–1920]), 2:27; *Warren-Adams Letters* (Massachusetts Historical Society, *Collections*, vols. 72–73 [1917–1925]), 1:186.

17. Mercy Otis Warren, *History of the Rise, Progress, and Termination of the American Revolution*, 3 vols. (Boston, 1805), 1:75–76; Gordon quoted in Allen French, *The First Year of the American Revolution* (Boston, 1934), 303; Emerson quoted in *Writing of George Washington . . .*, ed. Jared Sparks, 12 vols. (Boston, 1833–1837), 3:491. Although the Continental articles of war were not greatly different from those Massachusetts regulations previously in effect, Washington energetically enforced the new articles whereas Massachusetts General Artemas Ward had not. Likewise, Ward's general orders often did not seem to be disseminated to the lowest levels of command. As to both the articles and general orders, Washington practiced better communication and more vigorous enforcement than did Ward. Such practices were keys to much that he accomplished. For Ward's instructions to the New England army, see Massachusetts Historical Society, *Proceedings* 15 (1876–1877), 87–113.

18. Shy, *A People Numerous and Armed*, chap. 9, "The Military Conflict Considered as a Revolutionary War"; John Adams to Abigail Adams, July 30, 1775, *Letters of Delegates to Congress* 1:681.

19. John Adams stated that "the three Cardinal virtues of a Soldier" should be cleanliness, activity, and sobriety (Adams to James Warren, June 10, 1775, *Letters of Delegates to Congress*, 1:467). For Massachusetts's apprehension on quartering matters, see, for example, Joseph Hawley to Gerry, February 18, 1776, Austin, *Gerry* 1:163. Greene to Charles Pettit, November 23, 1778, *Papers of Greene* 3:81.

20. For some of Washington's most telling observations on provincial jealousies, see *Writings of Washington* 3:325–26, 451, 4:77. On officer appointments, see *Papers of Washington* 1:361. While Congress commissioned regimental officers, they were nominated by their own colony or state government. In time, a number of units were raised by direct authority of

Congress—including two Canadian regiments, a corps of invalids, and three partisan corps; however, these units were never more than a small percentage of the total army strength. Wright, *Continental Army*, lists and gives a short history of "every permanent unit of the Continental Army"; see "Lineages," 195–350.

21. As to the selection and ranking of Washington's general officers, John Adams complained that "I have never, in all my lifetime, suffered more anxiety than in the conduct of this business" (*Letters of Delegates to Congress* 1:503). Two recent articles cast new light on Arnold's treason and the American reaction to it: James Kirby Martin, "Benedict Arnold's Treason as Political Protest," *Parameters* 11 (1981), 63–74; Charles Royster, " 'The Nature of Treason': Revolutionary Virtue and American Reactions to Benedict Arnold," *William and Mary Quarterly*, 3d series, 36 (1979), 163–93. Washington expressed his doubts about Frye to Joseph Reed, March 7, 1776, *Writings of Washington* 4:382.

22. Richard K. Betts, *Cold War Decision Making* (Cambridge, Mass., 1979), 67, 242, 243.

23. Washington to the president of Congress, July 10, 1775, Washington to John Thomas, July 23, 1775, *Writings of Washington* 3:325–26, 358–62.

24. Washington to the president of Congress, September 21, 1775, ibid., 509; French, *First Year*, 507, 509. Some American generals and colonels also had their own individual companies.

25. Washington to the president of Congress, September 24, 1776, *Writings of Washington* 6:108.

26. Washington to the president of Congress, July 10, 1775, ibid, 3:327.

27. Ibid., 379–80, 486, 487; Higginbotham, "The American Militia: A Traditional Institution with Revolutionary Responsibilities," in *Reconsiderations on the Revolutionary War*, 90–92.

28. Gordon quoted in French, *First Year*, 520; Jonathan Trumbull to Washington, December 7, 1775, *American Archives*, 4th series, 4:213.

29. Washington to Reed, Washington to the president of Congress, November 28, 1775, *Writings of Washington* 4:121–22, 124.

30. On December 11, 1775, Washington informed the president of Congress that "the Militia are coming fast, I am much pleased with the Alacrity which the good People of this province [of Massachusetts] as well as those of New Hampshire, have shewn on this occasion" (*Writings of Washington* 4:156). Moreover, they performed far better than he had expected, in December at least (Ibid., 185). See also Greene to Jacob Greene, November 30, 1775, Greene to Nicholas Cooke, February 6,

1776, *Papers of Greene* 1:158, 192; Freeman, *Washington* 3:578–79. At the end of February, Washington still had 5,821 militia present and fit for duty (Charles H. Lesser, ed., *The Sinews of Independence: Monthly Strength Reports of the Continental Army* [Chicago, 1976], 16).

31. Washington to the president of Congress, February 9, January 4, 1776, *Writings of Washington* 4:315–18, 208. Perhaps because of the delicacy of the idea, the proposal in favor of extended enlistments was not entered in the journals of Congress. Another possibility is that the proposal may have been made in a committee of the whole and thus would not have appeared in the journals. On January 19, 1776, however, Richard Smith of New Jersey recorded in his diary: "A Motion that the new Troops be enlisted for 3 Years or as long as the War shall continue was opposed by the Northern Colonies & carried in the Negative." Bernard Knollenberg has noted that the initiative originated in Congress and not with Washington, as some historians had erroneously claimed. It is unlikely, however, that such a measure would have eventually passed without Washington's endorsement (*Washington and the Revolution: A Reappraisal* [New York, 1940], chap. 12). Washington first expressed the idea of seeking bounties and an army for the duration in a letter to Joseph Reed, February 1, 1776, *Writings of Washington* 4:300.

32. Washington's letter was taken up in Congress on February 22, 1776, the day it arrived from Cambridge, and it generated wide-ranging and intense discussion. Among the reservations expressed were fears that men would object to serving under officers from other colonies, that the assemblies might lose control over the nomination of officers, and that Americans would be averse to signing up for an indefinite period. According to James Duane of New York, Connecticut's Roger Sherman declared that "long enlistment is a state of slavery. There ought to be a rotation which is in favor of liberty" (*Letters of Delegates to Congress* 3:295). See also Richard Smith's diary entry for the same date (Ibid., 297).

33. Gerry to Horatio Gates, June 25, 1776, John Adams to Henry Knox, August 25, 1776, ibid., 4:313–14, 5:63; Samuel Adams to John Adams, August 16, 1776, *Writings of Samuel Adams* 3:310; Billias, *Gerry*, 71.

34. These points about Washington's relations with provincial leaders are nicely developed in White, "Standing Armies in Time of War," 147–58.

35. Most of the letters are in *Writings of Washington*, vols. 3–4 passim. Philander D. Chase of the *Papers of George Washington* staff assisted me by pointing out a number of relevant missives not included in the previous edition.

36. Houlding, *Fit for Service*, particularly chap. 9.

37. Piers Mackesy, "What the British Army Learned," in *Arms and Independence: The Military Character of the American Revolution*, ed. Ronald Hoffman and Peter J. Albert (Charlottesville, 1984), 193–94.

38. The highest number, 23,179, was recorded in the monthly returns for September, 1775 (*Sinews of Independence*, 6).

39. G. B. Warden, *Boston, 1689–1776* (Boston, 1970), 319.

40. Ibid., 331.

41. Hezekiah Niles, *Principles and Acts of the Revolution in America* (Baltimore, 1823), 149.

42. Washington to the Massachusetts legislature, March 28, 1776, *Writings of Washington* 4:441 (Italics mine).

THREE
The Revolutionary Tradition

1. Washington to John Augustine Washington, March 31, 1776, *Writings of Washington* 4:450.

2. Doubtless some scholars were influenced to think of the War of Independence in global terms because of World War II and subsequent conflicts. Only a few important examples of this literature are provided here: Eric Robson, *The American Revolution in its Political and Military Aspects* (New York, 1955); Piers Mackesy, *The War for America, 1775–1783* (Cambridge, Mass., 1964); William B. Willcox, *Portrait of a General: Sir Henry Clinton in the War of Independence* (New York, 1964); John Shy, *A People Numerous and Armed* (New York, 1976). See also Don Higginbotham, "American Historians and the Military History of the American Revolution," *American Historical Review* 70 (1964), 18–34.

3. *Papers of Washington* 2:257; *Writings of Washington* 3:441, 4:207, 3:451. Washington's relations with the rank and file are detailed in Freeman, *Washington* 2:372, 376–77.

4. *Writings of Washington* 9:389.

5. "Farewell Orders to the Armies of the United States," November 2, 1783, ibid., 27:224.

6. Joseph Plumb Martin, *Private Yankee Doodle: Being a Narrative of some of the Adventures . . . of a Revolutionary Soldier*, ed. George F. Scheer (New York, 1962), 195–96.

7. John C. Dann, ed., *The Revolution Remembered: Eyewitness Accounts of the War for Independence* (Chicago, 1980), 62.

8. *Writings of Washington* 11:329–33, 366. According to Washington's

aide John Laurens, Steuben understood that foreign officers were unpopular at the time. As Laurens informed his father Henry Laurens, president of Congress, "In an interview between him [Steuben] and the general [Washington], at which I assisted in quality of interpreter, he
declared that he had purposely waved making any contact with Congress, previous to his having made some acquaintance with the Commander in Chief, in order that he might avoid giving offence to the officers of the army, and that the general might decide in what post he
could be the most useful" (John Laurens to Henry Laurens, February 28,
1778, ibid., 329n). Washington had hedged his gamble with Steuben by
promising him little in the beginning and giving him relatively minor
duties initially. A congressional committee at Washington's camp had
refused to consider Steuben for the post of quartermaster general because
he was a mercenary and a "Foreigner" (E. Wayne Carp, *To Starve the Army
at Pleasure: Continental Army Administration and American Political Culture,
1775–1783* [Chapel Hill, 1984], 46).

   While urging Congress to proceed cautiously in hiring foreign officers,
he stated that "this representation does not extend to Artillery Officers
and Engineers." In particular, he felt that well-qualified engineers were
"absolutely necessary," since few Americans were competent in that field
(Washington to Richard Henry Lee, May 17, 1777, *Writings of Washington*
8:76).

   9. Quoted in Carp, *To Starve the Army at Pleasure*, 161, 162. Carp is also
the authority in the text.

   10. William G. Simms, ed., *The Army Correspondence of Colonel John Laurens in the Years 1777–8* (New York, 1867), 170.

   11. Wright, *Continental Army*, 140; *Writings of Washington* 4:80–81, 8:29.

   12. Greene to Washington, December 3, 1777, *Papers of Greene* 2:232;
Wright, *Continental Army*, 141; *Regulations for the Order and Discipline of the
Troops of the United States* (Philadelphia, 1779), 138, reprinted in Joseph R.
Riling, *Baron von Steuben and His Regulations including a Facsimile of the Origi-
nal* (Philadelphia, 1966).

   13. Wright, *Continental Army*, 145–46. Immediately prior to his resignation in 1783, Washington wrote to Steuben in praise of his contributions:
"Altho' I have taken frequent opportunities, both in public and private,
of acknowledging your great zeal, attention, and abilities in performing
the duties of your Office; yet I wish to make use of this last moment of my
public life, to signifie in the strongest terms my entire approbation of
your conduct, and to express my sense of the obligations the public is
under to you, for your faithful and meritorious Services" (*Writings of
Washington* 27:283).

14. Howard C. Rice, Jr., and Anne S. K. Brown, eds., *The American Campaigns of Rochambeau's Army*, 2 vols. (Princeton and Providence, 1972), 1:78, 152; Rice, ed., *Travels in North America in the Years 1780, 1781, and 1782 by the Marquis de Chastellux*, 2 vols. (Chapel Hill, 1963), 1:107, 114. If not all French officers shared such a positive impression of the American army, they were as a whole "generally favorable" toward their allies (Lee Kennett, *The French Forces in America, 1780–1783* [Westport, Conn., 1977], 118). A year later, encountering the American army in New York, the French noticed even more improvement in the Continentals' appearance. A story making the rounds of the American camp had General Rochambeau, after reviewing Washington's regiments, exclaiming, "You must have signed an alliance with the king of Prussia. These troops are Prussians" (James Thatcher, *Military Journal* . . . [Hartford, Conn., 1854], 312).

15. According to Robert K. Wright, Jr., of the U.S. Army Center of Military History, "we are just starting to do the quantification work to test out the hypothesis of shortages, and . . . most appear to be more temporary than myth provides, and to be related more to food/clothing items than to arms or ammunition" (To the author, October 13, 1984). His comments, of course, apply to all of American military history and not to a single war.

16. Greene to James Varnum, February 9, 1779, *Papers of Greene* 3:223; Lee to Peter Muhlenberg, August 1, 1776, *The Lee Papers* (New-York Historical Society, *Collections*, vols. 4–7 [1871–1874]), 2:186. Recent scholarship has devoted considerable attention to the tensions between the army and the various sectors of civilian life, although not all of the following historians give equal weight to the dangers posed by the military's different grievances: Richard H. Kohn, "American Generals of the Revolution: Subordination and Restraint," in *Reconsiderations on the Revolutionary War*, 104–23; Kohn, *Eagle and Sword: The Beginnings of the Military Establishment in America* (New York, 1975); James Kirby Martin and Mark Edward Lender, *A Respectable Army: The Military Origins of the Republic, 1763–1789* (Arlington Heights, Ill., 1982); Martin, "A 'Most Undisciplined, Profligate Crew': Protest and Defiance in the Continental Ranks, 1776–83," in *Arms and Independence*, 65–76, 143–44; Lender, "The Social Structure of the New Jersey Brigade: The Continental Line as an American Standing Army," in *The Military in America: From the Colonial Era to the Present*, ed. Peter Karsten (New York, 1980), 27–44; Royster, *A Revolutionary People at War*.

17. For a treatment of the Conway Cabal within the context of the war effort in 1777–1778, see Don Higginbotham, *The War of American Indepen-*

dence: Military Attitudes, Policies, and Practice, 1763–1789 (New York, 1971; reprinted Boston, 1983), chap. 9.

18. Particularly impressive in this regard are Jack N. Rakove, *The Beginnings of National Politics: An Interpretive History of the Continental Congress* (New York, 1979) and White, "Standing Armies in Time of War."

19. Carp, *To Starve the Army at Pleasure*, 87. The internal problems of the Confederacy are illuminated in Frank L. Owsley, *States Rights in the Confederacy* (Chicago, 1925); Emory M. Thomas, *The Confederacy as a Revolutionary Experience* (Englewood Cliffs, N.J., 1971); Robert F. Durden, *The Gray and the Black: The Confederate Debate on Emancipation* (Baton Rouge, 1972); Stanley Lebergott, "Why the South Lost: Common Purpose in the Confederacy, 1861–1865," *Journal of American History* 70 (1983), 59–74.

20. *Autobiography of Benjamin Rush*, 145.

21. Gates to Elizabeth Gates, September 22, Gates Papers, New-York Historical Society.

22. The last two paragraphs in the text draw on Don Higginbotham, "Military Leadership in the American Revolution," *Leadership in the American Revolution* (Washington, D.C., 1974), 105–6, 107. Timothy Pickering, who later turned on Washington because of his unwillingness to endorse the Newburgh Addresses, declared in May 1778 that "for attention to business perhaps he [Washington] has no equal" (Quoted in Gerald H. Clarfield, *Timothy Pickering and the American Revolution* [Pittsburgh, 1980], 46). It is sometimes forgotten that Washington corresponded frequently with junior officers, who also brought their problems to his immediate attention. A sampling of their letters is in Dennis P. Ryan, ed., *A Salute to Courage: The American Revolution as Seen Through Wartime Writings of Officers of the Continental Army and Navy* (New York, 1979).

23. *Writings of Washington* 14:28, 27, 10:362–65. A field-grade officer voiced equally strong sentiments on the evils of inactivity (Mark E. Lender and James Kirby Martin, eds., *Citizen Soldier: The Revolutionary War Journal of Joseph Bloomfield* [Newark, 1982] passim).

24. *Writings of Washington* 10:363–64, 11:284–86.

25. Ibid., 18:209; Freeman, *Washington* 4:622–23.

26. *Writings of Washington* 18:210–11.

27. Quoted in Edmund C. Burnett, *The Continental Congress* (New York, 1941), 531–32.

28. Washington also used his aides—for example, John Laurens, son of the president of Congress—to communicate to the lawmakers and also on occasion to the public. In more recent history the "backchannel," as it is sometimes called, has continued to exist in one form or another. It has

sometimes been used by ranking officers to get information to key persons in the executive branch rather than to members of Congress.

29. In January 1779, Congress endeavored to clarify matters by declaring that Washington's control extended over all the military departments. In some respects the implication of such authority had been present from his appointment in 1775. Certainly Congress's resolution did not dramatically alter Washington's relationships with other department commanders. There are obviously no perfect institutional solutions to command relationships. The subject of reform of the joint chiefs of staff—a case in point—has sparked considerable controversy in the 1980s. Moreover, some service secretaries seek, and sometimes acquire, more autonomy than others.

30. "Proclamation," January 25, 1777, *Writings of Washington* 7:61–62, 61n; Clark to John Hart, February 8, 1777, to Elias Dayton, March 7, 1777, *Letters of Delegates to Congress* 6:240, 414.

31. Washington to the Board of War, January 3, 1778, Washington to the president of Congress, January 5, 1778, "General Orders," July 5, 1775, *Writings of Washington* 10:253–54, 267, 3:312. There are many similar statements sprinkled throughout Washington's wartime correspondence.

32. Carp, *To Starve the Army at Pleasure*, 199.

33. James Duane to George Clinton, with enclosures, November 11, 1780, *Letters of Members of the Continental Congress*, ed. Edmund C. Burnett, 8 vols. (Washington, D.C., 1921–1936), 5:445–46 n. 6; William Bradford to Jefferson, November 22, 1780, enclosing "Proceedings of the Hartford Convention," *Papers of Jefferson*, 4:138–41. The possibility of Washington as a military dictator is mentioned by Carp, *To Starve the Army at Pleasure*, 203; White believes that Congress would have granted such power had Washington sought it ("Standing Armies in Time of War," 310).

34. Rakove, *Beginnings of National Politics*, 289–91; *Papers of Jefferson*, 6:90–92; William T. Hutchinson, Robert A. Rutland, et al., eds., *Papers of James Madison*, 14 vols. to date (Chicago and Charlottesville, 1962–), 3:17–19, 71–72.

35. Within the framework of its considered authority, Congress in 1779 had given Washington as much flexibility and autonomy as it thought possible (John Jay to Washington, May 10, 1779, *Letters of Congress* 4:203–4; Thomas Burke to the North Carolina legislature, August 1779, ibid., 368–69). Yet throughout Washington behaved prudently, interpreting his powers broadly only when necessary and at times acknowledging in regard to specific issues the need for congressional guidance. On March 3, 1776, he wrote: "I am not fond of stretching my powers." Should Congress say, " 'Thus far and no farther shall you go,' I will

promise not to offend whilst I continue in their service" (*Writings of Washington* 4:368). Those were usually "only in intricate and perplexing cases." At such moments he "wish[ed] that Congress would chalk a line for me to walk" (Ibid., 25:222, 223).

36. Ibid., 26:97.

37. "Notes on Debates," February 20, 1783, *Papers of Madison*, 6:265–66.

38. Washington to Jones, December 14, 1782, *Writings of Washington* 25:430. The commander in chief recorded similar concerns to Benjamin Lincoln, October 2, 1782, and to James McHenry, October 17, 1782, ibid., 226–29, 269.

39. Knox to Alexander McDougall, February 21, 1783, quoted in Kohn, *Eagle and Sword*, 27.

40. The last fifteen years have witnessed a substantial outpouring of literature on the army's discontent at Newburgh. The strong possibility of a coup attempt is the theme of Richard H. Kohn, "The Inside History of the Newburgh Conspiracy: America and the Coup d'Etat," *William and Mary Quarterly*, 3d series, 27 (1970), 187–220, which is the fullest treatment of the subject. Certain aspects of Kohn's thesis have been criticized, and Kohn himself seems to have refined his argument to the point of taking a more qualified position. (See Kohn, *Eagle and Sword*, 17–39; Kohn, "American Generals of the Revolution: Subordination and Restraint," in *Reconsiderations on the Revolutionary War*, chap. 7 passim; Paul David Nelson, "Horatio Gates at Newburgh, 1783: A Misunderstood Role. With a Rebuttal by Richard H. Kohn," *William and Mary Quarterly*, 3d series, 29 (1972), 143–58; C. Edward Skeen, "The Newburgh Conspiracy Reconsidered. With a Rebuttal by Richard H. Kohn," ibid., 31 (1974), 273–98). Skeen takes a very different view. He maintains there was never any organized effort on the part of the army dissidents and thus no "real danger that Washington would lose control of the army, or that the army would lose control of itself. Washington's reaction to the Addresses and his conduct during the entire affair have given historians the mistaken impression that some momentous crisis was averted. In fact, Washington was quashing a phantom conspiracy" (Skeen, *John Armstrong, Jr., 1758–1843* [Syracuse, 1981], chap. 1, quotation p. 14). Skeen's writings also stress the involvement of younger officers in the Newburgh Addresses. In other nations, however, particularly in the twentieth century, "hotheaded colonels" have often led successful coups, as General Kenan Evren, president of Turkey, reminded columnist Joseph Kraft (*Washington Post*, February 25, 1982).

41. There are slightly different versions of Washington's remarks, but they are the same in substance (Freeman, *Washington* 5:435, 435 n. 39;

James T. Flexner, *George Washington*, 4 vols. (New York, 1965–1973), 2:507.

42. *Writings of Washington* 26:211–34 passim, 268–72 (quotation on p. 226). According to Congressman Madison, "The steps taken by the Genl. to avert the gathering storm and his professions of inflexible adherence to his duty to Congress and to his country, excited the most affectionate sentiments towards him" ("Notes on Debates," March 17, 1783, *Papers of Madison* 6:348). For other positive reactions from Madison and his Virginia colleagues, see Madison to Edmund Randolph, March 18, 1783, Virginia Delegates to Benjamin Harrison, March 18, 1783, ibid., 353–56. Congressional action on commutation is in "Notes on Debates," March 22, 1783, ibid., 375, 377 n. 3; "Continental Congress Report on Half Pay to the Army," March 21, 1783, *The Papers of Alexander Hamilton*, ed. Harold C. Syrett and Jacob E. Cooke, 26 vols. (New York, 1961–1979), 3:301–3 and notes.

43. White argues persuasively that congressional concerns about half-pay were much broader than simply a fear of perpetuating military influences in the new nation, the view of most previous writers ("Standing Armies in Time of War," 323–24 n. 18).

44. Hamilton to Washington, February 13, March 17, 1783, *Papers of Hamilton*, 3:253–55, 292–93; Washington to Joseph Jones, March 12, 1783, Washington to Hamilton, March 4, 12, April 4, 1783, *Writings of Washington* 26:214–16, 185–88, 216–17, 292–93 (quotation on p. 293); Jones to Washington, February 27, 1783, *Letters of Joseph Jones of Virginia, 1777–1787*, ed. Worthington C. Ford (Washington, 1889), 99–100.

45. Royster, *A Revolutionary People at War*, 319.

46. Larry I. Bland and Sharon R. Ritenour, eds., *The Papers of George Catlett Marshall*, 1 vol. to date (Baltimore and London, 1981–), 1:644.

47. Royster, *A Revolutionary People at War*, 351.

48. Rochambeau quoted in Kennett, *French Forces in America*, 83; Trenchard quoted in John Phillip Reid, *In Defiance of the Law: The Standing-Army Controversy, The Two Constitutions, and the Coming of the American Revolution* (Chapel Hill, 1981), 108; James Varnum to William Greene, April 2, 1781, *Letters of Members of Congress* 6:41–42.

49. *Papers of Jefferson* 6:413.

FOUR

George Washington and George Marshall

1. Marshall penned an account of his service in World War I, but it was not published until long after his death: George C. Marshall, *Memoirs of My Services in the World War, 1917–1918*, with notes and foreward by James L. Collins, Jr. (Boston, 1976). It should also be noted that Marshall's second wife, Katherine Tupper Marshall, wrote a highly useful reminiscence, *Together: Annals of an Army Wife* (Atlanta, 1946).

2. Max Farrand, ed., *Records of the Federal Convention of 1787*, 4 vols. (New Haven, 1911–1937), 3:85, 86n.

3. Forrest C. Pogue, *George C. Marshall* (New York, 1963–), 1:323. Thus far Pogue has published three volumes of his magisterial biography of Marshall: *The Education of a General, 1880–1939* (1963); *Ordeal and Hope, 1939–1942* (1966); and *Organizer of Victory, 1943–1945* (1973). For Pogue's brief preliminary assessment of Marshall, see *George C. Marshall: Global Commander* (Harmon Memorial Lecture: United States Air Force Academy, Colorado, 1968).

4. Russell F. Weigley, "American Strategy: A Call for a Critical Strategic History," in *Reconsiderations on the Revolutionary War*, 33.

5. Charles W. Eliot, *Four American Leaders* (Boston, 1907), 33–56; Henry Cabot Lodge, *George Washington*, 2 vols. (Boston, 1898), 1:73, 75, 94.

6. Henry B. Carrington, *Washington the Soldier* (Boston, 1898); Matthew Forney Steele, *American Campaigns*, 2 vols. (Washington, D.C., 1909), 1:19; William A. Ganoe, *History of the United States Army*, rev. ed. (New York, 1942).

7. Emory Upton, *The Military Policy of the United States* (Washington, D.C., 1904), 66–67.

8. Russell F. Weigley, *Towards an American Army: Military Thought from Washington to Marshall* (New York, 1962), 111. Disappointed in the public's response to his ideas and suffering from ill health, Upton committed suicide in 1881. His book manuscript, still incomplete, circulated among ranking military men and was finally published at the instruction of Secretary of War Elihu Root during the Theodore Roosevelt administration.

9. O. O. Howard, "The Example of Washington," *United Service* 4 (1881), 505.

10. Richard H. Kohn, "The Greatness of George Washington: Lessons for Today," *Assembly* 36 (1978), 6, 28; James L. Collins, Jr., "George Washington: Statesman and Strategist," 6. General Collins graciously gave me a copy of his essay, which he read at the Organization of American Historians meeting in Cincinnati, Ohio, April 7, 1983.

11. *Time,* January 3, 1944. Freeman's remarks appeared in editorial form in the *Richmond News Leader* and were enclosed in Freeman to Marshall, December 30, 1943, Marshall Research Foundation Library, Virginia Military Institute.

12. T. Harry Williams, "The Macs and the Ikes: America's Two Military Traditions," *American Mercury* 75 (1952), 32–39; also in *The Selected Essays of T. Harry Williams: With a Bibliographical Introduction by Estelle Williams* (Baton Rouge, 1983), 173–81.

13. Samuel P. Huntington, *The Soldier and the State: The Theory and Politics of Civil-Military Relations* (Cambridge, Mass., 1957), 367–68.

14. Pogue, *Marshall* 1:189. Marshall himself stated, "It fell to me in the World War to actually write more detail orders, and to actually prepare orders for large forces, than I believe any officer in the Army" (*Marshall Papers* 1:438).

15. Henry H. Arnold, *Global Mission* (New York, 1949), 163–64, 172, 180, 187, 195. For Marshall's growing awareness of the importance of airpower, see *Marshall Papers* 1:676–79, 698–99, 707.

16. Omar N. Bradley and Clay Blair, *A General's Life: An Autobiography* (New York, 1983), 83–84; Pogue, *Marshall* 2:ix, 411. Eisenhower took Marshall at his word. See Joseph P. Hobbs, ed., *Dear General: Eisenhower's Wartime Letters to Marshall* (Baltimore, 1970), especially Hobbs's discussion of this point (pp. 83, 231). Eisenhower subsequently wrote that Marshall "insisted that his principal assistants should think and act on their own conclusions in their own spheres of responsibility, a doctrine emphasized in our Army schools but too little practiced in peacetime" (*Crusade in Europe* [New York, 1948], 35).

17. *Marshall Papers* 1:705. Marshall repeated such comments about Pershing in interviews with Forrest Pogue (Ibid., 189, 194, 200–1). The Marshall-Pershing relationship calls for further study, although it receives some attention in Pogue's work and also in Frank E. Vandiver's *Black Jack: The Life and Times of John J. Pershing,* 2 vols. (College Station, Texas, 1977).

18. Frederick Palmer, *Newton D. Baker: America at War,* 2 vols. (New York, 1931) 1:162.

19. For Marshall's temperament, see index references in Pogue, *Marshall* 1:417, 2:488, 3:676; for Washington's temperament, see index references in Freeman, *Washington* 4:727, 5:568. Katherine Marshall admitted that her husband's anger could be "like a bolt of lightning out of the blue. His withering vocabulary and the cold steel of his eyes would sear the soul of any man whose failure deserved censure" (*Together,* 109).

20. *Marshall Papers* 1:537.

21. Pogue, *Marshall* 2:111.

22. Washington's "Sentiments on a Peace Establishment" are in *Writings of Washington* 26:374–98.

23. John McAuley Palmer, *Washington, Lincoln, Wilson: Three War Statesmen* (New York, 1930); *Marshall Papers* 1:328–29, 333–34, 344–45, 347–48, 351.

24. This section of Marshall's report, entitled "For the Common Defense," is from "Biennial Report of the Chief of Staff, July 1, 1943 to June 30, 1945," in *The War Reports* (Philadelphia, 1947), 289–96. I have used a reprinted text in Walter Millis, ed., *American Military Thought* (Indianapolis, 1966), 436–45. Marshall's admonitions about standing armies and expenditures are found on 437, 439–40.

25. Quoted in I. B. Holley, Jr., *General John M. Palmer: Citizen Soldiers and the Army of a Democracy* (Westport, Conn., 1982), a splendid biography containing a wealth of information on the Marshall-Palmer relationship. For Marshall's references to Washington and to training and "not universal military *service,*" see *American Military Thought*, 436, 439, 440.

26. *Marshall Papers* 1:644; Holley, *Palmer*, 714.

27. *Marshall Papers* 1:644, 218, 222; Harvey A. DeWeerd, ed., *Selected Speeches and Statements of General of the Army George C. Marshall* (Washington, D.C., 1945), 36–39.

28. Quoted in Carl von Clausewitz, *On War*, ed. and trans. Michael Howard and Peter Paret (Princeton, 1976), 42–43.

29. Marshall made the same observation about "the political necessity for action" to a civilian audience: "The public demand it. They must have action. The party opponents utilize the lack of it to attack those in power. It presented a difficult business. The military staff workers, as a rule, do not fully appreciate this phase of the matter, if at all" (Speech to the National Institute of Social Sciences, May 18, 1949, Pentagon Office, Speeches, Marshall Research Foundation Library).

30. William C. Westmoreland, *A Soldier Reports* (New York, 1976), 159.

31. LeMay not only has endeavored to defend himself but has explained his interpretation of the proper relationship between civil and military authority in America (Curtis E. LeMay and MacKinlay Kantor, *Mission with LeMay: My Story* [New York, 1965]; LeMay and Dale O. Smith, *America is in Danger* [New York, 1968]).

32. Omar N. Bradley, *A Soldier's Story* (New York, 1951), 9.

33. Drew Middleton, "Vietnam and the Military Mind," *New York Times Magazine*, January 10, 1982, 34, 37, 82, 90, 92; Westmoreland, *A Soldier Reports*, 121.

34. Paul M. Kattenburg, "Reflections on Vietnam: of Revisionism and Lessons Yet to be Learned," *Parameters* 14 (1984), 42–50. The literature of

the Vietnam War has already reached floodlike proportions. A great deal of it has been discussed and analyzed in *Parameters,* the journal of the army War College. In addition to the Kattenburg article, I found the following particularly helpful for understanding critics of the American military: Guenter Lewy, "Some Political-Military Lessons of the Vietnam War, *Parameters* 14 (1984), 2–14, and John M. Gates, "Vietnam: The Debate Goes On," ibid., 15–25. The joint chiefs come in for further criticism in Lawrence J. Korb, *The Joint Chiefs of Staff: The First Twenty-Five Years* (Bloomington, Ind., 1976), 180, and in Betts, *Cold War Decision Making,* 35, 51. A much more sympathetic view of the military leadership is offered in Colonel Harry G. Summers, Jr., *On Strategy: A Critical Analysis of the Vietnam War* (Novato, Calif., 1982) and in Summers, "A Strategic Perception of the Vietnam War," *Parameters* 13 (1983), 41–46.

35. For an illustration, see Senator Joseph R. McCarthy, *America's Retreat from Victory: The Story of George Catlett Marshall* (New York, 1951).

36. A number of recent studies have significantly modified, to say the least, Huntington's interpretation of Gilded Age military professionalism: Richard C. Brown, *Social Attitudes of American Generals* (New York, 1979); Jerry M. Cooper, *The Army and Civil Disorders: Federal Military Intervention in Labor Disputes, 1877–1900* (Westport, Conn., 1980); John M. Gates, "The Alleged Isolation of the U.S. Army Officers in the Late 19th Century," *Parameters* 10 (1980), 32–45; James L. Abrahamson, *America Arms for a New Century: The Making of a Great Military Power* (New York, 1981), which contains the references to Sherman and Miles (31, 60, 74–75).

37. Pogue, *Marshall* 3:315; Dean Acheson, *Sketches from Life of Men I Have Known* (New York, 1959), 163–64.

38. *Marshall Papers* 1:613, 423, 659.

39. Ibid., 707.

40. Pogue, *Marshall* 1:307–8; *Writings of Washington* 11:291.

Index

Acheson, Dean, 135

Adams, John: on Southerners, 3; on standing armies, 49–50; on long-term enlistments, 62; on British regulars, 146–47 (n. 8); on Washington, 130, 147 (n. 13); "Cardinal virtues of a Soldier," 148 (n. 19); on ranking generals, 149 (n. 21)

Adams, Samuel: on standing armies, 50, 62

American military tradition, 1–6 passim, 38, 50, 55–56, 57, 58–59, 63, 100, 101, 106–38 passim

Amherst, Jeffery, 33

Arnold, Benedict, 3, 55, 95

Arnold, Henry H., 121

Bernard, Francis, 146

Betts, Richard K., 56

Bismarck, Otto von, 113

Blaine, Ephraim: on Washington, 77

Bland, Humphrey: *Treatise of Military Discipline*, 15, 18

Bland, Richard: defends Washington, 36–37, 145 (n. 48)

Boston: siege of, 44; population of, 66; British abuse of, 66; American liberation of, 67

Boudinot, Elias, 91

Bouquet, Henry, 18

Braddock, Edward: defeat of, 2, 8, 37, 106, 121; colonial criticism of, 10–11, 140 (n. 8); historical opinion of, 18

Bradley, Omar, 120, 121, 123; on military in a democracy, 131

Brandywine, 79, 93

British army, 19–32 passim; Braddock campaign, 8, 10–11, 15, 16; Cartagena campaign, 13, 14; wartime tactical training, 18; peacetime training of, 64–65; at Boston, 44, 45, 51, 52, 57, 66

Bunker Hill, 48, 49, 66

Butler, Benjamin F., 56

Byrd, William III, 22

Carp, E. Wayne, 85, 95

Carrington, Henry B., 111

Cartagena, 13, 14, 141 (n. 9), 141 (n. 12)

Chastellux, Marquis François Jean de, 80, 119

Chauncy, Charles, 11

Civil-military relations: French and Indian War, 33–40 passim, 54; British-American friction, 42, 46; first year of the Revolutionary War, 45, 46; civilian

Washington, George (*continued*)
78, 119, 123, 126; as a charismatic leader, 71–72, 121; fos-
ters nationalism, 72–73;
bravery of, 73–74; flair for the
dramatic, 74–75, 98–99; as
viewed by enlisted men, 75, 80;
as viewed by officers, 77–78,
80, 97, 119, 154 (n. 22); as
viewed by Congress, 80, 91, 94,
155 (n. 35), 157 (n. 42); opinion
of Congress, 86, 96, 97, 113,
129–30, 138; candid with Congress, 88–90; letters to Congress, 91–92, 99; jurisdictional
boundaries of, 92–94, 155 (n.
29), 155–56 (n. 35); policy of
impressment, 94–95; and Newburgh conspiracy, 98–100; on
hiring foreign officers, 152 (n.
8); compliments Steuben, 152
(n. 13); Constitutional Convention, 107–8; and historians,
109–13, 114–15; orders busts of
military heroes, 118; "Sentiments on a Peace Establishment," 124, 125, 126; and
"Ike" type generals, 125, 126,
128–29, 134, 135, 138; sensitive
to criticism, 131; on shared values, 138. *See also* Marshall,
George; Washington-Marshall
comparisons; Civil-military relations; Continental army
Washington-Marshall com-
parisons: Virginia, 107–8; decline to write memoirs, 107;
come out of retirement, 107; remote and aloof, 107–8; historians on, 115; honorary

degrees, 115–16; professional
experiences, 118–24 passim;
temperament, 123; political
sensitivity, 124–27 passim; view
of war, 127–28; Williams's
failure to treat, 116, 117, 128;
ignored by Huntington, 116–
17; compared to other generals,
129–30; candor of, 130–31,
133; on civilian-military com-
mon interests, 135–38
Washington, John Augustine, 69
Washington, Lawrence, 13, 14, 20
Wayne, Anthony, 3
Weigley, Russell, 110, 113
Westmoreland, William C.: on L.
B. Johnson, 131; sues Columbia
Broadcasting System, 132; *A
Soldier Reports*, 132
Whitman, Walt, 101
Wickham, John A., Jr., 133
Williams, Jonathan, 110
Williams, T. Harry: on "Mac"
and "Ike" leaders, 116, 117,
118, 128, 129, 138
Winchester (Virginia), 24
Wood, Leonard, 122, 131
World War I, 82, 119, 120
World War II, 70, 82, 93, 119, 151
(n. 2)
Wright, Robert K., 79, 148 (n.
15), 153 (n. 15)
War College: Historical Section,
128
Ward, Artemas, 3, 148
Warden, G. B., 66
Warren, James, 49, 50, 52

Yorktown, 80